CRESTED BUTTE

From Coal Camp
to Ski Town

By Duane A. Smith

WESTERN REFLECTIONS PUBLISHING COMPANY®

Montrose, CO

ISBN-13: 978-1-932738-06-3
ISBN-10: 1-932738-06-1

Library of Congress Control Number: 2005933544

Cover and text design: Laurie Goralka Design

First Edition
Printed in the United States of America

Western Reflections Publishing Company®
219 Main Street
Montrose, CO 81401
www.westernreflectionspub.com

To

Richard L. Gilbert

Table of Contents

CRESTED BUTTE
1910

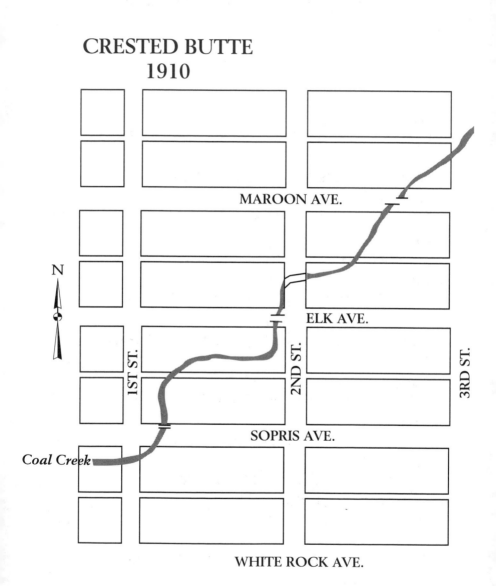

Map VII

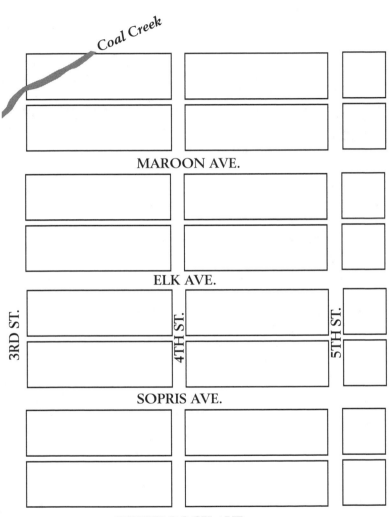

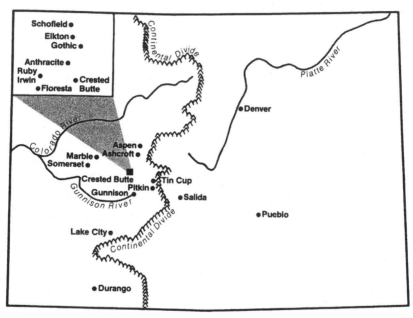

Reference map of early development in the Crested Butte area.

Preface

2005

"The reports of my death are greatly exaggerated," Mark Twain cablegrammed to friends in America in 1897 upon hearing that his illness had caused rumors. That would just as easily describe Crested Butte after its coal mining era ended. Just as Mark had many years left, so did, and so does, and so apparently will, this captivating hard-rock camp turned coal camp turned ski resort.

Crested Butte reached the grand old age, for a mining camp, of 125 years in 2005. Certainly, settlers were in the valley before that time, but the community was incorporated in 1880 starting its evolution toward the future.

Crested Butte, with its fascinating and unique evolution, deserved its story to be told. *Coal Was King: A History of Crested Butte, Colorado 1880-1952* originally appeared in 1984 an offshoot of the Mount Emmons project. That edition stopped with the closing of the Big Mine and the end of the coal mining era. Since that time the community has evolved and transformed itself once more. What folks had long cursed, or considered at best a hindrance, now is blessed, and this time nature provided a renewable endowment — snow.

This new edition incorporates the original, with a few corrections, and adds a chapter and an epilogue to discuss the past fifty plus years. Crested Butte has changed since the 1950s, but again that American icon, Mark Twain, has something to say to the twenty-first century: "What, then, is the true Gospel of consistency? Change."

My sincere thanks and appreciation to Jan and David Smith, who gave me the opportunity to bring Crested Butte's history into the twenty-first century.

Duane A. Smith
June 2005

Preface
1984

There is an old saying about coal mining: "God made the coal, then he hid it. Then some fool found it and we've been in trouble ever since."

Certainly Colorado coal mining has been lost to history for too long, and it is a goal of this study of Crested Butte to help rectify that injustice. Coloradans are poorer because the story has not been told.

Crested Butte was, and still is, a fascinating community. Having evolved from a hard-rock camp to a coal mining town, it is an unusual landmark in the saga of Colorado mining — or anywhere else for that matter. One might be tempted to claim this circumstance as unique, but not enough research on coal has been done to substantiate that fact.

Americans tend to make legends out of things they want to believe. We have tended to glorify the gold and silver camps, while ignoring the immigrant and company-dominated coal communities. This is one reason that the Crested Buttes of the West have not been seriously examined; there are, of course, many other reasons. No matter, coal towns and districts plainly do not exude the glamour and excitement of their hard-rock cousins. They have not been restored as tourist attractions, nor have they been credited with being major contributors to the state's development. To correct this historical misconception is another aim of this book.

If coal was the heart of Crested Butte, its people were the soul. They came to settle, to seek a fortune, and usually to move on, but for a while — sometimes a lifetime — they made Crested Butte home. Nowhere will their names be found as pioneers or statesmen, but they contributed while they lived, laughed, worried, dreamed, failed, and succeeded in a beautiful valley in the Elk Mountains. Consider them carefully, for their like will never be seen again.

The original research for this volume was done under contract with Centuries Research Inc. as part of the larger Mount Emmons Project funded by AMAX. My sincere appreciation goes to Steve Baker, Centuries president, for his cooperation and assistance. AMAX and CF&I Steel both have been most generous in their support of my research and eventual publication. Individually, CF&I Steel's Rich Yates and AMAX's Stanley Dempsey, David Delcour, Ken Paulsen, and Ron Saunders assisted in many ways, and my thanks go to all. Colleagues Lee Scamehorn and Duane Vandenbusche again generously shared their knowledge, and Jackson Thode kindly allowed me to use his photographs. Jon Raese and Jean Goldberg of the Colorado School of Mines Press skillfully transformed manuscript into book.

Finally, a deep debt of gratitude is owed to the Crested Butte people who shared their lives: John Somrak, Lyle McNeill, Frank and Mary Yelenick, A.J. Mihelich, John Krizmanich, Ruth Chappell, Whitey Sporcich, and Esta Gibson.

Two people especially helped make this book possible. Without my wife Gay it might still be languishing on my desk; her support, incisive comments, typing, and editing again proved invaluable. Longtime dear friend, enthusiastic photographer, and fellow softball devotee Richard Gilbert has taken photographs for several of my books. This time he caught the spirit of a coal mining community and its people before they were lost in the wake of a new generation and another era. To him this volume is dedicated.

CHAPTER 1

Hard Rock to Coal Town
1880-1892

For Crested Butte there would never be a summer quite so wonderful as the one of 1880. Optimism and confidence permeated the young community and the surrounding mining district. The Ute question moved swiftly toward resolution with the removal of the Indians to the west, out of the state, thus clearing all land titles and ending this barrier to permanent settlement and development. Investors were captivated; rich mineral discoveries seemed more commonplace than extraordinary, settlers and miners daily swelled in numbers, and even the transportation/isolation handicap looked to be on the road to a solution as the railroad neared. Crested Butte and the Gunnison Country had attained a certain status in the mining world.

Surrounded by a treasure trove of minerals, it seemed that Crested Butte could not fail to emerge as the most important mining community in the Elk Mountains. An unknown correspondent, writing to the *Denver Tribune* early in the year, had predicted such an evolution: "Crested Buttes [sic] is destined to be the great entrepot for all this section of the country." Now the visions of 1879 were becoming reality; Crested Butte stood on the threshold of blossoming into another Leadville.

Its prospects did not go unrecognized at home. City government was organized, with such familiar faces as Howard Smith and George Holt on the board. Mayor Holt had migrated from Leadville, exhibiting his confidence in the new community. Ambitious, with eastern connections, he was a man to keep an eye on. A name familiar to pioneer Coloradans also appeared; George Jackson, who on a long ago January day discovered gold near Idaho Springs and helped give foundation to the 1859 Pike's Peak gold rush, briefly resided in Crested Butte. No new fortune met him, and he soon moved on. The more numerous stable residents oversaw a growing camp, with lots selling briskly and merchants arriving to give credence to the "great entrepot." Telegraph connections, acquired in mid-August 1880, ended the communications isolation and demonstrated Crested Butte's progressive nature. Not many Midwestern farming towns could boast of so much progress so early in their careers.

The Crested Butte Town Company saw profit in all this prosperity, and it responded by grading streets, building side-walks, and preparing more lots for sale. It was advertise or die, and this community chose to live. Crested Butte was described as the "pleasantest location," where prospectors, speculators, and tourists "will find the best place for their headquarters." Smith and Holt energetically promoted the town company's interests and sold shares, a goodly portion of them going, via Denver and Rio Grande Railroad officers, into the portfolio of the Durango Trust, which at the moment was involved largely in establishing the town of that name. No more confidence in the future could be inspired than by this display of interest on the part of the railroad.

The hum of activity went on all summer and into early fall. Lumber mills could not keep up with the demand. Smith's addi-tion was already laid out, adjoining the old town to the east. The advent of a Sabbath school was unarguable evidence of a for-ward-looking attitude. Most encouraging was the fact that an unusually large percentage of the settlers were women and chil-dren. A bright employment market featured higher wages than in most settled areas: carpenters commanded $3.50, bricklayers $5, and blacksmiths $4 per day. Only those unafraid of "healthy manual labor" need apply, however. Prices were more reasonable than might have been expected for a new, isolated mining dis-trict — another good omen. It was hoped Crested Butte might become the county seat. (Its luck did not hold there.)

Even celebrities visited Crested Butte. Former President Ulysses Grant and party arrived in August on a tour of Gunnison County's principal mining camps. They came and departed, returning to Manitou Springs where Mrs. Grant had remained, then journeyed on to Denver. Grant had been favorably impressed; the *New York Times*, August 16, 1880, reported that the vast coal deposits had been "critically examined by General Grant, and pronounced by him to be of unusual extent and value." Bust those buttons!

Other visitors of lesser fame also reached Crested Butte, and their impressions have likewise been preserved. Traveler and author Robert Strahorn came after Grant, collecting material for a soon-to-be published pamphlet. He waxed eloquent about the "village" of 300 souls, romantically located in a beautiful meadow stretching to the mountains beyond. He saw nothing but promise — not surprisingly, since he wanted to sell his pamphlet locally and boost sales abroad. U.S. Deputy Mineral Surveyor Thomas Ingham described the town's extensive building activity and lot speculation and its potential as a smelting center. He spent more time than Strahorn in the nearby mining camps, particularly Irwin. Many visitors that year seemed more interested in silver than in prosaic coal and what it portended for the future of Crested Butte, shown clearly by the coverage Gunnison County received in the prestigious New York Engineering and Mining Journal. The period from July 1880 to June 1881 included twenty-two articles on Gunnison, only one of which mentioned Crested Butte.

Locally and statewide, though, the town held its own, particularly when locals took pen in hand and started writing letters. One signed "Mac," for instance, communicated to the *Rocky Mountain News* on July 28, 1880, how accessible the town was, its lovely location in the "most beautiful valley" of the state, and the joys of the dust-free, cool days and nights. There was no reticence when it came to promoting one's home. Becoming somewhat of a prophet, "Mac" concluded: "Though at present none are here for their health, yet I think that in the near future this place will rank among the leading sanitariums of the Rocky Mountains." No less bold was a correspondent to the *Denver Times:* "No one cognizant of the facts relative to this place, and familiar with the causes that contribute to the rapid and permanent growth of our western mining towns hesitates to rank Crested Butte as the 'future great.'"

Despite such puffery, as the year ended Crested Butte remained, like several score of its contemporaries, only a mining camp with the potential for permanence. To the question: "Would it last?" The answer was a resounding "yes." It contained the basic ingredients that guaranteed the permanence all mining communities hoped to attain. Its business leadership was strong, aggressive, and backed by outside capital. They were aided in their struggle for economic survival by a central location for a supply point. Coal's prospects intrigued the Denver and Rio Grande, which could bring to fruition the promise of railroad connections without which a camp would wither and die. Already appreciated, albeit untapped, were the tourism possibilities of a beautiful site and an invigorating climate. In spite of its high elevation, Crested Butte's climate was milder than the surrounding mining camps; it was an obvious wintering place for those who did not care to brave a Rocky Mountain winter at its worst in the high country. The potential for nearby ranching and agriculture remained unrealized at the moment, but it was real and assured a diversified local economy. All told, Crested Butte was blessed. Only Gunnison, of its neighbors, would provide any long-range challenge.

As in other western mining districts in 1880-81, rivalry prevailed among small communities scratching and clawing to gain an advantage. Irwin, for instance, had the audacity to call Crested Butte a "little one-horse town." Crested Butte entered the fray early with an 1881 promotional pamphlet. Care was taken, it was claimed, not to overstate the facts, "as the truth in the case is so extraordinary as to be almost incredible to strangers." Take that, Gunnison, Gothic, Irwin, Elkton, Schofield, Pittsburg, and even Ashcroft and Aspen! The insulted ones retaliated; Gothic's *Miner* pointedly stated on April 16, 1881, that the pamphlet had been kept from the "sight" of its citizens, and Crested Butte should not lie and claim all the surrounding towns and mines as its own. For shame! Gothic soon dropped by the wayside along with all the rest, except Aspen and Gunnison. The former almost blossomed into a second Leadville, completely overshadowing the Gunnison Country and becoming famous as an entity unto itself. Crested Butte was small fish beside Aspen. Gunnison and

Crested Butte bickered back and forth for decades. In 1886 their feud descended to the level of who had the best July Fourth celebration.

In the end, the hard-rock mining camps faded and died, and only Crested Butte survived as a coal town. Helen Hunt Jackson saw the future in her August 1883 visit (August became a favorite month for visits — the weather was best and the snow danger least): "When the wilderness has proved a mockery, refusing to give us its treasures and the miners have pushed on, leaving behind them no trace except deserted cabins and mounds of tin cans, the names they gave still ring." She saw a few camps in full bloom, but most were in old age:

> It is hard to keep separate the fantastic and the sad in one's impressions; hard to decide which has more pathos, the camp deserted or the camp newly begun, the picture of disappointment over a past or that of enthusiastic hopes nine out of ten of which are doomed to die. I have sometimes thought that the newest, livest, most sanguine camps were the saddest sight of all.

The two primary components of continued prosperity and growth were transportation and development of the supply point concept. The first resolved itself easily with the coming of the Denver and Rio Grande, which stopped its tracks right at Crested Butte, giving the community an almost unbeatable advantage. Even before the rails arrived, local merchants took advantage of their windfall and worked hard to improve roads leading out to consumers; they intended to make Crested Butte a transportation and supply hub.

With Gunnison County financially unable to undertake an extensive, costly road building program, the burden fell to individuals, who responded vigorously with toll roads. Surveys in 1880-81 lined out the routes, and private enterprise rose to the task; roads went to Gothic, Irwin, and some of the mining basins. Holt and Smith eventually became owners of the road to Irwin and were able to keep it open year-round, a major accomplishment. Weather bedeviled them, as did declining revenues, and this toll road went the way of all others that were not simply abandoned; the county purchased it in 1890 for $600.00. The county commissioners finally had two roads built over the mountains to Ashcroft/Aspen to tap that market. Pearly Pass proved a failure. For a while Maroon Pass steered some supplies and ore to and from Crested Butte, but it was a far too round-about route, which fell victim to the railroad's reaching the thriving Aspen district.

Even with improvements and continued construction, the roads never satisfied everyone, either going to the wrong place, not maintained, too steep, too narrow, or (most likely) demanding too high toll charges. Complaints and downright anger over maintenance aside, the roads did tie Crested Butte into all the nearby districts. It was not unusual on a summer day to see between 100 and 200 burros in and near Crested Butte, ready to pack supplies or bring ore out of the mines. One late summer day in 1885, the editor of the *Elk Mountain Pilot* estimated there were 600 burros. He must have guessed at the number by the noise they generated — that many would have almost outnum-bered the residents. Freighting was a big business in the eighties; the community became to the mines of the Elk Mountains "what Boston is said to be to the rest of the universe, the Hub." As Helen Jackson observed, "that one fact alone [is] an excellent reason for being."

Snow, deep snow, snowdrifts — these facts of high altitude life were something with which road builders, travelers, freighters, miners, and everyone else had to learn to live. As the pioneers quickly discovered, it snows long and hard in and about the Elk Mountains, and keeping the roads open involved a relentless battle. Holt and Smith solved part of the problem by not charging a toll in the winter, allowing the traveler to make his way over those roads that could be maintained after a fash-ion. Winter retained its stranglehold despite the best efforts of puny man at shoveling, dragging, pushing, and digging. Deep snow, fresh snow, and snowslides threatened travelers and freighters, stopping travel and business for weeks, occasionally months, on end. Sleighs carried passengers, mail, and some small express items, but stages and wagons stopped for the season. In the spring the annual opening process began again, and winter's persistence was measured by the date the roads could handle wagons. Like the mountain flowers, it was a positive sign of spring when wheeled vehicles appeared on Crested Butte's streets. One ingenious Crested Butte inventor devised a machine for forming roads and paths "upon bodies of snow." Although he was granted a patent, the invention never succeeded — Winter was King!

That irrepressible *Elk Mountain Pilot* editor of the eighties, John Phillips, believed that no more healthy place could be found, and deep snow did not necessarily mean extremely cold weather. One either learned to use snowshoes (skis) or stayed at home, he flatly stated. Others, at the moment, did not look upon snow so benignly.

Winter or summer, Crested Butte's merchants were willing and eager to do business. Unlike the neighboring smaller communities where a catch-all general store, along with a blacksmith shop, saloon, and boarding house might compose the whole business district, Crested Butte showed signs of diversified development early and soon displayed a respectable district. Specialized businesses appeared; dry goods, drugstore, jewelry, bank, "tonsorial artists," bowling alley, grocery stores, and meat markets gave the town a depth that Gothic, for example, could never match. Add to these attorneys, doctors, restaurants, saloons, hotels, blacksmiths, mining engineers, newspaper, and coal dealers, and a picture of the mid-eighties comes into focus. Mix in the railroad connection, local lumber mills, and the smelter; and the business foundation emerges. By 1890 there were also, among other things, eight saloons, two barbers, more drug stores, groceries, meat markets, and restaurants, one gent's furnishings, a milliner, laundry, livery, furniture store, shoemaker, photographer, bank, hardware, blacksmith, and stationery store — a representative sample of the business community of nineteenth century America.

None of these enterprises was more important to Crested Butte's present and future than the newspapers, whose varied careers reflected the fortunes of gambling on the economics of Colorado business life. During the eighties the *Gazette* and *Republican* were born and died after a short life, unable to survive in the limited advertising and customer market. Much more significant and long lived was the *Elk Mountain Pilot*, which John Phillips removed from the nearly dead camp of Irwin in May 1884. The *Pilot* would stay "in the ring," as Phillips called it, as Crested Butte's principal newspaper until mid-1949.

The *Republican* made its debut on October 5, 1881, with a broad statement that explained what the editor intended to accomplish with his press and pen:

Why does Crested Butte want a newspaper? We'll tell you why. Because there is more to be told about her that the world outside wants to know, than can be said of any town in the Gunnison country.

She has greater natural resources.
More gold and silver mines.
More anthracite coal.
More coking coal.
More steam coal.
Better business prospects.
Better climate than any town in the county can claim.
And yet, she is almost the least known because she has no newspaper. Her resources have not been overlooked, it is true. They have been kindly taken in and cared for by the neighboring camps.
Gunnison claims her coal.
Irwin claims half her mines.
Gothic the rest.

Pugnaciously and confidently, he launched his publishing venture. Crested Butte would seldom be voiceless or overlooked in the world of journalism.

Not content with that opening blast, the editor went on to explain further why a newspaper was needed, even demanded:

We have opinions of our own and want to express them.
We have matters of interest to tell and want to make them known.
We have work to do and must be about it.
Our principles are Republican, not the weakly, washy subterfuge called "Independent."
Our purpose is to work for the best interests of all our people, without any limitation or reservation whatsoever.
Furthermore we have come to stay.

He was right on all counts but the last, staying would be hard. Crested Butte's newspapers served all these areas and more. They became a vital facet of the community's life, its promoter, and defending avenger. Let no one tread on Crested Butte!

The newspapers reported the spice of life that makes history. The more personal, free-wheeling journalism of Colorado in the 1880s kept the community and its people on their toes. For example, over the years editors took after a "measly lot of Gypsies" pestering the town, decried the overabundance of carousing canines, advocated establishment of a public library, and supported postage rates ($.02 per letter!). They forever reminded subscribers to pay their overdue subscription bills, or admonished holdouts to subscribe to "save borrowing from your neighbors." Newspapers, without doubt, faced a hard fight to keep the wolf from the door. And as the town gadfly and defender, they occasionally stomped on someone's toes. The *Gunnison Review-Press*, on February 16, 1884, had taken all it was going to take and leveled its heaviest ink at the "little insipid" *Gazette*: "They have shown themselves below the recognition of men." Unfortunately, the reason for such condemnation is lost to history.

John Phillips, the outstanding editor of this era, moved to Crested Butte from Irwin, where he had founded the *Pilot*. This Philadelphian had previously worked in his home town, and in Minnesota and Texas, before his penchant for wandering took him to Silver Cliff in 1879. From there to Irwin and finally Crested Butte were only minor jumps; frontier newspaper editors were a transitory lot. Even rivals admitted his paper was carefully edited and "always interesting;" he could ask no higher accolades.

One of the most interesting things about this man is that long after he had moved on from Crested Butte and finally retired to California, he retained a lively interest in his old home. Well into the 1930s, his peppery and fascinating letters occasionally appeared in the *Pilot*, telling how it was back in the "old days."

Besides a newspaper, every Colorado mountain town worth its "grit" needed a "fine" hotel, at which the visitor would find a cup of good steaming coffee, wholesome meals, and fresh linen, white like the "fresh driven snow." An aspiring community had to be sure to put its best culinary and lodging feet forward. The town company undertook to provide just such a place; the Elk Mountain House was formally opened with a grand ball in

February 1882. The sumptuous supper, featuring oysters, cold turkey, chicken, salads, cakes, and fruits, sent all the dancers home satiated and content, even though the gentlemen so out-numbered the ladies that the extras were forced to serve as "wall-flowers." The fifty "handsome rooms, all plastered and elegantly furnished" stood ready to receive guests at the corner of Elk Avenue and Fourth Street.

The Elk Mountain House was not Crested Butte's first hotel. The Forest Queen Hotel predated it, going back to 1880. Although it was called a "credit" to such a young community, the Forest Queen changed hands several times and was soon eclipsed by its new rival.

A town aspiring to permanence needed a bank, and Crested Butte secured one, courtesy of Colorado's silver millionaire, Horace Tabor. At the height of his financial power, bedrocked by the outpouring of Leadville's silver, Tabor invested in Colorado's financial institutions — becoming one of the state's leading bankers. Always eager to invest in a new region, Tabor helped underwrite the Bank of Gunnison and, as would be expected of Colorado's best known mining man, purchased the Augusta Mine up in Poverty Gulch. Not satisfied, he backed the Bank of Crested Butte, opening its doors on August 9, 1881, amid the editorial bouquets of the *Gunnison Review*, which congratulated its "sister city" on the "accession of a first class banking house." Tabor served as nominal president, his name more prominent than his presence. The auspicious start did not mean Tabor would stay interested in Gunnison County. His investments there got lost in the shuffle as he plunged ahead with unlimited faith in Colorado's future. Tabor finally sold his interest in the Crested Butte bank in May 1884, thus ending his banking venture there. The bank continued to give the town a financial advantage over all of its neighbors, except Gunnison. Tabor was gone but not forgotten. Phillips recalled years later, with no disrespect, that "Old Man Tabor" was the meal ticket for many in those days.

Equally fortunate for Crested Butte were those noisy but essential lumber mills, the town that boasted a lumbering operation drew customers for timbers, boards, lath, shingles, and other wood items. While buying these items, they were easily tempted to do the rest of the week's shopping. Eventually, it was hoped, these folks would form the habit of coming into town, even if there was no lumber on the shopping list. In the lumbering industry, George Holt was in the forefront. With his New York-born partner, V.F. Axtell, he gained control of the two local lumber mills. Blessed with nearby heavy timber stands, Holt and Axtell developed their lumbering business into one of Crested Butte's economic pillars of the eighties. At one time they owned lumberyards there and at Irwin, closing out the latter when the camp and its mines declined. So prosperous was the lumber business that they finally closed their general store (they were entrepreneurs of the first rank within Crested Butte's definition) and concentrated solely on lumber.

Twenty-eight-year-old Chicagoan George Holt journeyed to Crested Butte in June 1880 from Leadville, leaving behind a mixed career as manager of the Little Chief Mining Company. The smelter he built proved to be a lemon, costing his backers a small fortune. What experience he had to undertake mine management and smelter construction seemed limited at best, perhaps nonexistent. He and Axtell, who had also once lived in Chicago, opened a general merchandise store and ventured into the lumbering business — a natural for Holt, who had grown up in his father's Midwestern lumber firm. Holt was drawn to Crested Butte by coal and silver mining interests, which also led him to invest farther north in the Hahn's Peak Mining district. His appetite for speculation seemed insatiable.

Holt's Leadville experience with the Little Chief, in which he had been a minority stockholder, somewhat dampened his enthusiasm for mining, and he eventually turned to more mundane pursuits. Plenty of Crested Butte opportunities beckoned him. He dabbled in the town company, toll roads, and general merchandising before focusing on lumbering. It was just the type of life this energetic businessman loved. His sister Ellen pictured her brother as a man who did not have much time for recreation, always being intent on his various businesses. A westerner described him in more earthy terms: "Most men who come out here rest on the train, work like hell when they get here, and rest going back. But Holt, he works like hell all the time." Crested Butte suited perfectly a man of Holt's drive and vision. He set out to carve an empire for himself. Single and with money behind him, he could not help but achieve success, as it was defined by nineteenth century business America.

Holt and Axtell dominated Crested Butte's business in the first half of the decade; both seem to have been good businessmen. Less is known of the older Axtell, but it is certain that Holt had the courteous, jovial personality needed by the successful western businessman. Never would these two have the field to themselves, however, as others were also drawn by Crested Butte's potential.

The Metzler brothers, Samuel and Victor, arrived in the mid-eighties to assume control of the bank. Sam came first from their Ohio home to Irwin and then to Crested Butte. His younger brother joined him later, and for nearly a quarter of a century they handled local banking matters, earning a conservative, honest reputation for their business dealings. Victor married a Vermont girl in 1887 and brought his bride to Crested Butte. In a story that sounds as if it came right out of Owen Wister's *The Virginian*, two Vermont ladies were reported to have been outraged:

> *I do not think it right to allow that big westerner to carry off Miss May [Sowles], who is the life of our social set; just graduated from college, a fine musician, whose long line of ancestry fought in all the colonial wars.... Why, they tell me, that only a few years ago, the Indians were killing people in the very town the Metzlers are going to live in!*

Their worries were for nothing — by the time Miss May stepped off the train, Crested Butte's uncivilized frontier days were over.

Enticed by the potential of the West, Herman and Louis Glick, Cleveland businessmen, liquidated their store there and traveled to glittering Leadville in 1879. To their dismay, they found themselves too late; others had already been lured to the "Silver Queen" by the same idea. Undaunted, they moved to another "equally promising" district, Gothic. By this time their aspirations exceeded the reality, and they wisely turned to Crested Butte in 1880. For the next thirty-nine years their store on Elk Avenue offered a variety of goods. They had trod a long emigrant road from their native Hungary.

For these six men and their contemporaries, Crested Butte represented a rung on opportunity's ladder. Some stayed there all their lives; others, like Holt, who left in 1886 to return to Illinois to become a successful lumber and businessman, continued their search. The west promised much, but did not always fulfill that promise. Faith, ambition, and a willingness to gamble on an unknown future were things all of these men had in common.

If it were possible to sketch a composite picture of a Crested Butte businessman, he would have been in his middle or late thirties, Midwestern born, and probably married; so said the census taker of 1885. The foreign-born merchants all emigrated from England, Germany, France, Hungary, or Canada. The Colorado census of that year gives an interesting statistical look at the Crested Butte people from all walks of life.

Most were American-born; Pennsylvania, Illinois, New York, and Ohio led the way. Only a scattered number of New Englanders would have greeted Miss May when she arrived on her honeymoon. She would have found, to her delight, a larger number of married couples than usual for a Colorado camp of this era. The British Isles (England, Wales, Ireland, and Scotland) contributed the lion's share of the foreign contingent. Thus a common language and cultural heritage predominated in this hard-rock mining camp, which was slowly metamorphosing into a coal community. Crested Butte, at the time, still looked much like its neighbors, hardly recognizable as a coal town in the typical sense.

In mid-1885 miners were nearly equally divided between coal and silver; however, had the census been taken earlier or later in the year, instead of in June, the former would have surged to the front. The transitory coal miners moved on during the slack summer period, perhaps changing their occupational identification by dabbling in silver mining. The professional community consisted of three physicians (at least one of whom was the company doctor), three lawyers, one minister, and a mining engineer — not exactly what Miss May had left behind in Vermont.

Mary Willison typified the women of Crested Butte. This wife and mother had moved there in 1882 and become active in the United Congregational Church and various community projects. Not many other activities included women, who did not achieve the right to vote in Colorado, except in school elections, until 1893. They overwhelmingly listed "keeps house" as their occupation. Those not so identified reported other occupations typical of the late nineteenth century: dressmaker, teacher, cook, laundress, servant, manager of a boarding house, and (not so common) telegraph operator; the last was Mary Axtell, V.F.'s daughter. She must have been a remarkable young lady because she also served for a time as assistant postmaster. More characteristic was the tribute given by the *Republican* on July 5, 1882, to Mrs. J.C. Stearns, one of the first lady pioneers, whose home was always open to the sick and unfortunate and "whose many acts of love and charity" were gratefully remembered.

With due regard to Victorian sensibilities, census takers did not enumerate prostitutes, though they plied their profession. Economically, the greatest impact of women was as homemakers, no easy task when the cost of living exceeded family income. Except for teachers and a few exceptions like Mary Axtell, the working women were relegated to low-paying service occupations, not management or professional positions. This reflected male reluctance to admit them into other areas, not lack of ability or ambition.

Crested Butte was never overwhelmed by a surplus of women, in 1885 they composed 28.6 percent of the population, a percentage that slowly increased. Two-thirds of the 216 women in Crested Butte that June were fifteen years of age or older, providing the nucleus of Miss May's new friends. No matter how one looked at it, though, Crested Butte had been and would remain a man's world. Nevertheless, women like Mary Willison were subtly shaping the community more to their tastes. They had come a long way since 1879 and would persist in their efforts in the years ahead.

Few non-whites made any headway in Crested Butte. Former slave, fifty-five-year-old Wayman Boyd was an exception — he operated a barber shop nearly twenty years, before leaving in 1901 to return to his native South Carolina. A host of friends saw this "honest and good old gentleman" off. One Chinaman, who attempted to open a laundry in 1884, found himself hung in effigy and fled before someone tried the real thing. Crested Butte opened as and continued to be a white, American/northern European community.

This ethnic picture changed as the decade waned and the nineties opened. Where Scotsman John Gibson had once favored hiring his own countrymen to labor in the mines under his supervision, to work from "wassal to wassal" (whistle to whistle), now he saw names like Kochevar, Pasic, and Golobich beginning to appear on the company payroll. Then came the strike of '91, which made it obvious that there were more eastern Europeans than previous sources had indicated. To reach their American dream they still had to overcome discrimination and cultural hurdles; newspapers took little notice of them, except for such incidents as an 1890 fight between two Italians in which one was killed.

The community where these people lived and worked was being molded into the image of their previous homes. They undertook little innovation, wanting only something similar to their cherished memories. Hence Crested Butte, snuggled in the Elk Mountains, reflected primarily the characteristics of middle class American society.

Evidences of this character were numerous. Every town must have a public school. The first and second buildings were frame; an aspiring community could do better and did in 1883 with the Rock School. Residents could point with pride to this substantial school, built to be permanent. Appearance proved to be more important than substance. Several times during the decade, a shortage of funds nearly closed the school (and did so in 1885); teachers never complained of being overpaid. This being one of the few professions open to women, they did not demand equal pay for equal work. A man served as principal of the school with the title of professor, which sounded impressive. The newspaper pointed with pride, for example, to Professor W.A. Clark: "Our people are to be congratulated on having secured such a man for principal of the school." Businessmen dominated the school board over the years, and they saw to it that there was not waste and that a solid "3 R's" education was instilled in the students.

Equally important to the community's cosmetic appearance was a church and a steeple with a bell to ring out the good news. Crested Butte wanted it known that it was a civilized, Christian town. The Episcopalians gained an early toehold, only to lose out to the Congregationalists. First came a Sunday school, then plans for a church. A bell, but no minister, arrived for the new church in the spring of 1882. The members found it hard to attract a man to this small and financially struggling congregation, which encompassed all the Protestants in town: Methodists, Episcopalians, and Presbyterians. It took them years to complete their "edifice." The *Elk Mountain Pilot* finally chided its readers (April 16, 1885) that it was too bad a town of that size still had no completed church building. Support for the structure was more vocal than financial. The Union Congregational overcame such handicaps and provided an excellent social and leadership outlet for women, a Sunday school for children and adults, and a variety of community programs.

The Catholics, relegated first to the city hall for their services, soon found their numbers increasing, and they, too, were determined to have church building. St. Patrick's resulted, and its role in Crested Butte steadily increased in the 1890s.

A school, churches, and a city hall gave credence to Crested Butte's claim of respectability. Businessmen watched over each carefully, for they knew that what was good for the town's image was good for their business. As a result, names such as Holt, Smith, and Metzler appeared on the rolls of the council or as mayor. Construction of a city hall was almost as important to the "skyline" as the church steeple. Discussion of the subject led finally, in 1884, to the completion of the hall and a grand ball to celebrate the opening. Everyone was agreed on such a positive addition, and the city fathers earned universal praise. They also drew their share of brickbats over bad streets and town indebtedness, as well as other problems as they erupted. Their primary task, however, was to pass and amend ordinances and generally keep town government functioning, which they did with as little fanfare and expense as possible.

The one major catastrophe with which the city fathers had to deal was a January 25, 1890, fire that destroyed much of the community's business district. They had prepared for just such a dreaded occurrence, not uncommon in the mining West, as best they could. Waterworks had been constructed (1883-84) and volunteer fire companies organized. When not busy fighting fires, the fire laddies sponsored dances and other fundraisers to keep themselves going. The Gazette praised them as boys who "are always on hand when they are needed."

On this particularly cold, windy winter night the firemen could do nothing. The "new" waterworks were not finished, forcing them to throw snow on a fire roaring out of control before they arrived. The snow and wet blankets saved some buildings, but fifteen were destroyed, including four owned by the Metzler brothers, the post office, and the entire north side of Elk Avenue between Second and Third. Crested Butte rebuilt, although water to fight fires would remain a problem; attempts to keep the pipes from freezing were an annual winter battle.

When the federal government was mentioned in late nineteenth century America, the post office came quickly to mind. Even as early as 1880, complaints were prevalent about delays which, at that time, were understandable. Later complaints were more justified. Snow and snowslides tormented Uncle Sam's boys as they went on their appointed rounds, stopping them completely on occasion and killing at least one carrier on his way to Aspen in 1885.

Crested Butte created few political ripples. Not enough votes were tallied to do more than slightly influence Gunnison County races, which themselves hardly carried any weight statewide. Politics in this day and time percolated as part fun, part serious business, and part pure devilment. Phillips recalled the 1884 presidential election at the Smith Hill coal mine: a local Democrat exchanged straight Republican party tickets for Democratic ones, while purchasing drinks for everyone "on the house" as a cover.

While the evolving community pattern was a familiar one of imitation, examples of a progressiveness, more evident in western than in Midwestern or eastern communities, also emerged. The telephone reached Crested Butte in 1882, offering private lines between any two points — store/residence, office/mine, and so forth — at "the same rates as other parts of the state." Seven years later, electric lights brightened the town's streets. "Quite an improvement," commented the *Elk Mountain Pilot*. The idea that the town should be beautified also persisted, long before such ideas were fashionable. The *Republican*, April 26, 1882, asked, "What is this by the Bank? It is a tree. Will the tree grow? Yes." It went on to encourage the planting of more trees. They would, the editor explained, "enhance the value of your property." Like others of their generation, some residents unthinkingly littered trash and dumped garbage wherever they pleased, creating a sickening stench and unsightly, noxious trash piles. These conditions kindled the ire of the newspapers and the more fastidious residents, but to no avail.

The Crested Butte Town Company watched over its handiwork. Its officers advertised and promoted to the effect that their lots would appreciate in value with increased settlement. Donating lots for the church and school and building a hotel (Elk Mountain House) further enhanced their financial prospects.

Officers and directors Howard Smith, George Holt, and William Holt shrewdly offered only every alternate pair of lots for sale, at a "low price," and promised purchasers that money received would be expended on improvements of a "public character." They planned to realize their own profits from the remaining lots.

The Durango Trust also owned lots, and from its reports can be traced the progress of the Crested Butte Town Company's aspirations. In 1884 the Durango Trust reported no yield from its investment because the company put most of its receipts into the hotel, which had not returned a profit and was sold on "long time." Two years later, it reported dejectedly that the parties involved deemed it best to prorate the liabilities and wind up the Crested Butte Town Company. The investors were not to fear, however; Crested Butte was a "flourishing little mining town," and the 322 lots that the Durango Trust received would be a bonus.

By 1888 only two additional lots had been sold, unfortunately. Other large holders of town property had abandoned most of theirs, rather than pay taxes on them, which did not augur well for the future of the trust's lots. The 1890s proved no better for land sales, and the Durango Trust made its profits on coal and lumber.

What had gone wrong? The Trust candidly admitted that the town did "not grow or prosper," laying the blame on the extremely cold winters and deep snow. Obviously Crested Butte never grew as expected, partly because the local hard-rock mining had quickly faltered and faded, partly because of isolation and climate, and partly because coal mining seemed so mundane. The founders had oversold its prospects and dreamed an impossible dream; Crested Butte would never be another Leadville, or even come close to it. Sales of town lots languished predictably, though vigorously promoted with various incentive. It almost seemed un-American when land sales failed to lead one down the road to fortune.

Crested Butte's development was not really all that bad. Its slow but steady growth was much preferred to the boom-and-bust cycle of its neighbors. Even though it never lived up to the "magnificent outlook" of '81 or produced company profits, the town had not done badly. The building boom peaked in 1880-81, having adequately provided for local needs. For the rest of the decade the community stabilized and prospered within the limits afforded it. It promoted itself unabashedly, even though challenged by an imposing lineup of Colorado rivals which could also entice with a scenic location, healthful climate, and a host of natural resources, but without Crested Butte's geographical isolation and chilling reputation for severe winters.

To their credit, Crested Butte folk never lost their faith or optimism in the eighties. They were assured that next year would bring improvement — with spring would come something better, if they could just wait it out. They agreed with Helen Hunt Jackson, who fell in love with the site and its "wild and picturesque" scenery. It would be, she wrote, a rash man who would undertake to set a limit on the natural resources of the area.

While they waited for the promised millennium, Crested "Butteians," as H.H. (Mrs. Jackson) called them, enjoyed themselves. With food-laden tables they celebrated July Fourth and Christmas/New Year — men, women, and children all participating in the festivities. Labor Day became more important after the Colorado Assembly officially recognized it in 1887. No one could feel socially deprived in the midst of the variety of available diversions, from picnics and fishing in the summer to sleigh rides and dancing schools in winter. Add concerts, weddings, a literary society, visits, surprise parties, and oyster suppers, and one begins to get an idea of the town's social season. Nineteenth century Americans could be classified as enthusiastic "joiners," and for them there were such lodges as the Odd Fellows, Masons, and the Ancient Order of Hibernia. For the graying boys of '61, there was the Grand Army of the Republic.

The athletically inclined were not ignored. Their activities and interests ranged from football (which caused its first injury in 1890 when Henderson Fossett dislocated his shoulder while kicking (!) a ball) to horseracing. Roller skating, something of a fad at different times, particularly attracted the younger set. Baseball was the sport, however; the town's reputation hung on the success of its team. A game could come to violence, as in June 1886, when Gunnison defeated Crested Butte 24-18 amid wrangling and turmoil. Each rival newspaper blasted the other community. Gunnison sharply criticized Crested Butte fans for their "indecent abuse" of the umpire and also for delaying the game for twenty minutes to watch a dog fight on the diamond! Crested Butte complained about the unsportsmanlike conduct of the victors, who paid a Grand Junction pitcher twenty-five dollars for the game. A rematch brought even more humiliation: the local nine lost that one 26-4.

A more lasting claim to fame can be made for Crested Butte in the realm of skiing — it was one of the Colorado spots where skiing really took root. (It would have been called snowshoeing then.) For once the prodigious amounts of snow proved a blessing. As early as the winter of 1880-81, the boys were making "snow show runs" down mountainsides for a purse of twenty-five dollars. Other "meets" attracted skiers from Gunnison, Irwin, Gothic, and elsewhere during the decade. Mishaps, such as broken legs, forecast what was to come, as did the fact that in 1883 Irwin earned a bit of notoriety by playing baseball in November on "snow shoes."

For warm-blooded sportsmen who did not care to venture out in the six months or more of winter, Crested Butte provided its share of saloons, gambling halls, and a small red-light district. In this milieu, amid the companionship of one's friends, a comfortable social evening could be enjoyed, even if the Union Congregationalists disapproved. For a bachelor, the saloon and its environs were home away from home; for respectable ladies the area was strictly off limits. Nowhere else provided entertainment and sociability for the transitory miners and others who spent a season or two out of their lives in Crested Butte.

Reformers grieved over, and town fathers winked at, the red-light district. It stimulated business, but it also caused trouble. Crested Butte's first murder was committed here, and it was the site of the possible first suicide, one Frankie Gorman. The city fathers received a complaint in April 1885 about prostitutes and responded typically by appointing a committee to select a proper place to locate their houses. Selection by rejection exemplified nineteenth century zoning. Actually, though, Crested Butte's red-light district never attracted the same attention as those of other mining communities. The town's slow growth and the larger number of families kept it within bounds, and it never achieved fame as the "brothel heart" of the Elk Mountains.

Crested Butte, with its successes and failures, was the permanent and preferred home for a substantial number of its residents. They found living in the mountains more costly, as would be expected; even the benevolent Denver and Rio Grand charged high freight rates. Occasionally though, such as in the winter of 1884, locals could point with pride to the fact that apples by the barrel were costing less there than in Denver. Most of the time they could count themselves lucky if they held even. For instance, in 1892, potatoes were selling for $.02 a pound in both the capital and Crested Butte; eggs sold for $.25 per dozen, $.04 higher. Those who yearn for the good old days, at least its prices, would consider bread at three loaves for $.25, sugar at six pounds for $.50, and coffee at $.30 per pound real bargains. But not many would trade today's improvements for the lack of indoor plumbing, cold outhouses, epidemics without a cure, dust and coal soot, the ever present fire danger, painful dental visits featuring foot pump drills, childhood deaths from now easily curable diseases, no electricity, and the refuse and permeating stench.

Crested Butte in the 1880s and early 1890s evolved from a camp typical of Colorado mining communities into a coal town, but it never became a "typical" coal community. Its hard-rock beginnings insured that would not happen. Colorado Coal and Iron never dominated Crested Butte as it did other of its coal camps, nor did a company store rival the main street merchants. It might have been the major employer, it might have wielded the economic clout, but Crested Butte was not its town.

There was some discussion, however, about just how much influence the company had. The Durango Trust (1886) accused it of controlling the business of the town, "which tends to check independent enterprise and growth." And the *Gunnison Review Press*, the year before, charged superintendent James Robinson of trying to "influence" voters, i.e., his workers. The Trust was obviously upset over its failure to sell lots, but how much the company could be blamed for this is questionable. And the fact that the paper used the word "influence," rather than a stronger one, says much. However, where smoke rises some fire smolders, and time would tell the tale.

Crested Butte was moving well into its second decade by 1892. Even though it had not lived up to the "great success" Howard Smith forecast for it back in December 1880, it had survived, put down roots, and promised to maintain itself in the years ahead. That was success enough for the past years. One had only to look around Crested Butte and see the remains of camps that had failed. Holt, Smith, and others could be proud of the permanence they had achieved.

CHAPTER 2

Coal Becomes King

1880-1892

L onely William Howe did more than just describe Crested Butte and vicinity to his faraway family. As he chronicled his 1880 Colorado journey, his business eye saw a future for the town. That future lay with a smelter that would "no doubt [be the] life of the place." He commented further on the coal mines, observing that they produced a "very good grade" of bituminous. Spring-heartened residents, if they had been privy to his letter, would probably have concurred with his predictions and observations. Smelters and coal mining seemed to hold the keys to the future. They would have gone one step further and added hard-rock mining to the list of possibilities. The three were locked inextricably: mining yielded the ore, which had to be reduced to bullion; the smelter needed coal to generate power to work the ores. If all went well, Crested Butte's future was secure; it would not decline and disappear as had the multitude of other mining camps which had preceded it on the Colorado urban stage, only to decline and disappear. Three cheers and a tiger for Crested Butte!

The best laid plans often go awry — the future would not evolve that easily. When it came to hard-rock mining, the community and district had been living largely on hope. There had been some silver and a touch of gold excitement in 1879, and it was assumed that the next year could only be more prosperous

— the Gunnison Country was the talk of Colorado, perhaps greater even than Leadville. It did not happen that way. Production, which rose to the $600,000 range by 1883, never climbed any higher, hardly better than what one of the big bonanza mines was capable of doing in an off year.

Crested Butte sat in a good spot to reap the benefits from its tributary Elk Mountain mining district, Washington Gulch, Irwin, O-Be-Joyful Gulch, and others, but large deposits were not being found. Many reasons were proposed. Miners complained about isolation, transportation costs, and the need for a smelter that returned profit to the miner, rather than a situation under which smelting expenses equaled or were more than the value of the ore. Some grumbled about the harsh climate, long winters, and deep snow; however, as newspaper editor John E. Phillips commented, it was just as convenient to mine underground in the winter as any other time. Shipping supplies and ore presented other problems. There also existed a continuous need for outside investors to pump money into future bonanzas; the Gunnison Country had a hard time attracting them. All these factors together meant that hard-rock mining was in trouble.

No one worried too much, though, because other Colorado mining districts had survived similar problems in their early days and gone on to prosper; so would Crested Butte, whose districts offered glorious prospects and an unprecedented future. Crested Butte newspapers throughout the eighties boomed their local mines and districts, always expecting that the mining surge was near. The *Gazette*, October 6, 1883, published a typical comment:

Why no one can conceive what a bright future is before us. Poverty Gulch alone will make this one of the most substantial towns in all Colorado, to say nothing of the other gulches around us. We are satisfied to wait results, and we know full well that another season will develop greater things.

Another season? More than one passed — 1884, 1885, 1886 — and each was similarly depressing. Things got even worse after mid-decade, when production slumped to the $100,000 range, hardly enough to seduce outside interests and investors. Hiawatha, El Paso, Forest Queen, Augusta, Sylvanite, Milwaukee, and Daisy are names of mines that scarcely evoke a remembrance today, yet they all had their moments of glory and earned a few laudatory newspaper comments.

Talk was cheap; exploration, development, and production costly. They all led to a great deal of fleeting hope, always high in the spring when men had forgotten last year's disappointments after a winter of creating rich veins in their mind's eye. The *Gazette*'s frustrated editor finally exploded in early May 1886 that if there was mineral, it was time to get it out, to show the outside world "there is more in our statements than idle talk." His bombast did not help; the promising start dwindled away. Hard-rock mines would never bedrock Crested Butte, despite continued prospecting and casual production that extended well into the twentieth century.

Before they fell into the dump of history, some of these prospects were visited by noted author Helen Hunt Jackson, up from Colorado Springs on one of her forays into the mountains. She had been to the rich and famous, the small and declining districts and knew mining better than most women of her generation. Her comments appeared in the *Atlantic Monthly*, December 1883, under the intriguing title "O-Be-Joyful Creek and Poverty Gulch."

She saw the irony of it all and put her finger on one of the eternal truths of mining:

> *Poverty Gulch and O-Be-Joyful Creek — the two will be found always side by side, as they are in Gunnison County. Only a narrow divide separates them, and the man who spends his life seeking gold and silver is as likely to climb the wrong side as the right.*

Of course the prospector/miner was always convinced that he was climbing the right fork in the trail. That dream kept western mining pulsating for several generations. Mrs. Jackson saw coal outcroppings and was told of mountains full of silver and gold. "What more," Jackson philosophized, "could the heart of the money lover ask, and what plainer indication could nature give of the chief duty of man in lands thus formed and filled?"

Some of what she saw depressed her. Far ahead of her time, Jackson questioned the compatibility of a field of purple asters with the sight of men digging, coking, and selling coal across the stream, men who were blind to the beauty at their feet. Or the foaming, splashing, sparkling O-Be-Joyful Creek, the same one that separated aster and coal — the prospectors hammering away high above cared nothing about maintaining its purity, unless it was needed to drink. There was no accounting for such differences, she concluded, "no adjusting them, either, unluckily." The basic conflict she pinpointed would ring down through the years. Jackson predicted that ten years from then the coal bank might not pay, but "I shall have my aster field."

The hope of becoming a smelter center evaporated with the failure of mining's development. Miners liked to blame the lack of a smelter for the demise of mining — without a smelter to work low grade ores profitably, the mines could not be developed. What they were unwilling to admit was that it took a steady ore supply to operate a smelter profitably, something that never came from Crested Butte's neighbors after 1882. Howard Smith and his Iowa Mining and Smelting Company tried their best to combine mining and smelting in one operation and develop coal as well. Their twelve-ton capacity plant could not survive, even with an advantageous location. High costs of transportation, an unstable ore market, perhaps poor management, and the region's general isolation in 1880-82 doomed the effort. By the mid-80s, Crested Butte had only a sampler to test the ores for nearby mines. But the idea for that smelter center did not die.

In the end, Smith and his fellow investors were right in one out of the three bets they made: coal came through for them. Not a bad ratio for mining investment in a new area. While prospectors invaded the mountains in search of their bonanza in silver or gold, a few more farsighted, practical men filed claims on the coal banks in the valley. They plainly saw the wave of the future for Crested Butte, in spite of the heated excitement over the precious metals and discoveries of marble and iron.

Unlike gold and silver, coal does not fire men's minds, especially not in the silver-charged Colorado of the 1880s. The fact that Crested Butte's deposits tested equal to the best of Pennsylvania, the measure of quality for the era, was irrelevant. There existed a need for coal and coke (bituminous coal from which volatile constituents have been driven out by roasting, producing a product known for its heat producing quality) as fuel for homes, mines, smelters, businesses, industry, and railroads. The existence of both anthracite (hard) and bituminous (soft) coal deposits around Crested Butte was unusual and extraordinary, but hardly as exciting as the prospects for silver. It seemed more prosaic than profitable that Crested Butte was noted as early as '81 for its "wonderful coal banks" rather than as a mining camp surrounded by rich ores.

As a result the stampede passed it by, leaving coal to be developed by Smith, Leadville smelterman and future Colorado governor James Grant, and the Denver and Rio Grande Railroad, which needed the coal and planned to tap the Gunnison mining districts. Writer Robert Strahorn reached Crested Butte in August 1880, reporting that the railroad already controlled 1,000 acres of coal land. Coal mining had advanced to the point of having a tunnel 200 feet along one vein. Some of the bituminous coal was already being turned into coke by roasting it in heaps in the open air near the mine. The coke gained local renown, being especially prized by blacksmiths in their work. Strahorn just missed seeing the first shipment of coke headed for Leadville smelters over roads that sometimes beggared that description. The *Elk Mountain Pilot*, located at nearby Irwin, went so far as to predict in the December 9 issue that next year coal mining would almost equal silver mining. That took some audacity — hard-rock miners did not often deign to mention coal and precious metals in the same breath. If transportation problems could be overcome, the anticipated millennium might arrive.

Coal is a bulk shipment item and needs the cheapest, year-round transportation available. That translated easily at this time into the railroad. Hence railroads, which obviously were prime customers as well as principal carriers, came early to be associated with coal mining. What better way, in the nineteenth century entrepreneur's mind, to cover all bets than to have the railroad own the coal mines? The profits would roll in uninterrupted.

If a mining district, or for that matter a community, hoped to achieve permanence, it must have railroad connections; nothing else would do. Even before coal emerged to intensify it, that dream existed. Some enterprisers talked of doing it on their own, and in this way the Crested Butte and Grand River Railroad Company got as far as filing incorporation papers with the Colorado Secretary of State before collapsing. More important,

Colorado's own Denver and Rio Grande had its eye on Gunnison and Crested Butte. In 1880 the rumor of its interest became fact. The *Gunnison Review* (September 11) predicted that now was the time to buy town lots. They might also have advocated coal land, but most of it was already gone.

The immediate goal of the railroad was Gunnison, the county seat. The D&RG could not be at all sure of getting there first, because the Denver South Park and Pacific had cast its eyes in the same direction. Rio Grande President William Jackson Palmer need not have fretted; his company won the race by crossing Marshall Pass and reaching Gunnison on August 8, 1881, while its rival was expensively hung up driving the Alpine Tunnel. Beyond Gunnison beckoned Crested Butte, an easy valley grade away. Those isolated souls could hardly wait; nor could Gunnison, which faced the prospect of an early winter coal shortage (and resulting high prices), until the mines were reached. By mid-November the tracks neared Crested Butte, and plans were afoot to lay track through town to the anthracite mines beyond. The glorious day, November 24, finally came, when the station opened for freight and passenger business. Denver was now only a day's trip away. The world awaited Crested Butte coal. The entire Elk Mountain district stood to profit, since stage connections could be made for Schofield, Gothic, Irwin, and all other points. Gunnison breathed a sigh of relief as the coal trains started to roll. Three boxcars and thirteen carloads of coal arrived on November 29.

Already Crested Butte seemed changed. The railroad's coming "has transformed that place from a rather dull sleepy hamlet into a thrifty and enterprising town," admitted the *Elk Mountain Pilot*. Next season would certainly see the tracks extended even farther. What a future lay ahead!

Like marriage, not everything lived up to expectations. Most of the branch lines that were planned to reach such camps as Gothic and Irwin never materialized, although tracks did extend beyond Crested Butte to the anthracite mine of Smith Hill. A new railroad depot in '83 somewhat salved local feelings; the D&RG considered the old one too small for the volume of business transacted. Some trouble over railroad rates flared in 1884 after the railroad came under a new presidency and different control, the somewhat visionary Palmer having resigned. The favorable position the Colorado Coal and Iron Company (controlled by Palmer and friends) once enjoyed was temporarily threatened by these changes, before the situation improved.

Crested Butte, simply a pawn in a game for high stakes, sat on the sidelines and watched. The town and the railroad needed each other, if each hoped to make a profit on local operations. Necessity will bring oil to all sorts of friction. Equally disturbing in the long run was the D&RG's switch to broad gauge on its main lines, particularly into Leadville. The Crested Butte line remained narrow gauge, necessitating eventual transshipment from narrow to broad gauge cars and raising transportation expenses. This problem vexed Crested Butte; company and residents clamored for a broad gauge connection, seen as a glittering savior enticingly near yet just out of reach.

With practical foresight, the Denver and Rio Grande moved to consolidate what it already had before worrying about what lay ahead. Palmer and his associates had consolidated several earlier companies into the Colorado Coal and Iron Company in December 1879. Bold plans stood behind this consolidation, of which coal and coke were only two ingredients. Town promotion and speculation and iron and steel manufacturing were other parts of it. Already nearly 100,000 acres of land fell under their control, including coal lands in Fremont, Huerfano, and Las Animas counties. The company's coal production approached half of Colorado's total. Standing pat was not a part of these entrepreneurs' plans; they continually acquired coal lands, and Crested Butte eventually became a part of their empire. What it offered that they did not already have was anthracite and, as a bonus to their coal holdings, and the latter provided a source of fuel for the mountain smelters, particularly those at Leadville. Crested Butte eagerly anticipated welcoming the predicted 500 men who would be employed in mining and coking during the upcoming winter. Coal mining was seasonal, the most active periods being fall, winter, and early spring. This was a convenience that left plenty of time to prospect for precious minerals — Crested Butte could have its cake and eat it, too.

A wonderful year 1881 had turned out to be. Silver mining reached new heights, gold mining was reviving, the railroad arrived, and coal's destiny seemed secure. The future had already come. Investors from Chicago, New York, and Philadelphia would soon be there — the world knocking on the door. "In these great blessings, no place in the United States can compare with Crested Butte!", crowed the *Republican* on October 5, and no one dared deny the statement. Crested Butte held a royal pair in coal and silver; no other Colorado district, nor even other Rocky Mountain states, could claim similar endowments. That silver would one day falter mattered little; the anthracite and bituminous together were good enough to hold their own. Colorado Coal and Iron stood ready to exploit the region's full potential. One of the first signs of development was the sight of horses pulling coal-loaded cars from the mines, with the contents being stored at the dump for eventual rail shipment. Boarding houses constructed near the mine provided convenient lodging and made the walk to work an easy one on snowy days (for which the district gained early fame). By year's end anthracite from Crested Butte had reached Leadville, Pueblo, and Denver.

In the decade ahead the enthusiasm of that year was borne out, although overeagerness occasionally carried some folks too far. Crested Butte never developed into a new Pittsburgh; its planned iron furnaces, to be complemented by an immense steel mill at Gunnison, never illuminated the night skies. But these deficiencies caused no consternation — plans of Colorado Coal and Iron promised enough.

The initial available market was the western part of Colorado (just opening to settlement as the Utes were being removed to a Utah reservation), the mountain towns (particularly Leadville), and local areas. Beyond, Utah beckoned with a strong potential coke trade, once the D&RG completed its line. Farther west lay the vast Pacific slope with its undeveloped potential. Even Denver's *Rocky Mountain News* (November 28,1882) applauded: "This part of Gunnison county is the Lehigh Valley of the west." Convinced of the wisdom of its investment, Colorado Coal and Iron, within a year, owned and leased over 2,000 acres in and around Crested Butte, partly, to be sure, as a defensive measure against the encroachment of other railroads. The company would not brook any competition; with railroad and coal acreage in hand, it controlled Crested Butte's coal for all practical purposes. Within four years of its birth, this erstwhile hardrock camp had evolved into a corporation-supported community, if not quite the company town of coal legend.

Mining moved ahead rapidly in 1882-83, with no significant setbacks. Although barely beyond the development stage, Crested Butte had become the major mountain coal community and was considered to be one of the "comers" in Colorado. Bituminous production, centered at Crested Butte, easily surpassed anthracite from neighboring mines.

After open pit experiments had proved the suitability of the coal, Colorado Coal and Iron moved rapidly to establish coking operations on a permanent basis. Believing that no coal found on the Western Slope could compete with the Crested Butte product, the company in 1882 underwrote the construction of fifty beehive ovens, so named because of their shape. Within a year, fifty more were authorized. Without question, coke produced in them was superior to the open pit variety because of better control over the process and less waste. The ovens, build in a long chain, had railroad tracks running past their doors for ease and efficiency of handling. Wheeled right out of the mine and into the oven, the coal was then heated for forty-eight to seventy-two hours to drive off impurities, the number of hours depending on the coke quality desired. The process produced, along with dense clouds of smoke and soot, a product preferred by lead-based smelters.

Crested Butte was only part of the Colorado Coal and Iron production. Unrivaled by western competitors, who were handicapped by transcontinental freight rates, the company was challenged primarily by eastern competitors. Colorado ranked fifth in coke production in 1885-86, behind Pennsylvania, West Virginia, Alabama, and Tennessee. Nor was Crested Butte the Colorado coke king; El Moro's 250 beehive ovens, located near Trinidad, far surpassed it in production.

Twenty-four additional coke ovens, built in 1884, raised the total capacity to 1,000 tons per month, not bad for this young district. Although extolled for their initial construction (the *News* especially hailed the use of Golden's fire brick over rival Pueblo's), the beehive ovens, nevertheless, needed repairs in 1885 to make them more "durable." Perhaps the heavy snowstorm back in '82, which hampered but did not stop work (to much local acclaim), somehow flawed the structures. This small setback caused hardly a misstep in Crested Butte's march to further glory, nor did it diminish its claim as a coal mining center.

More construction followed, so that, by 1892, 154 ovens sat lined up in rows. Tracks capped the brick tops, over which horses dragged cars loaded with coal from the mines to be dumped and fired in furnaces below. Several days later, coke was drawn from the ovens into railroad cars waiting on the tracks. Low in ash content, Crested Butte coke commanded a premium price on the market, which stretched, if not yet from the Mississippi River to Pacific Coast, at least from Salt Lake City to Denver and Pueblo. Around the ovens bustled a crew of sooty, sweaty workers, bedeviled by heat and smoke in the summer, which even Crested Butte's elevation could not alleviate, and the unusual combination of extreme cold and intense heat in the winter. Never considered the equal of mining *per se*, in either status or pay, working the ovens gave many new immigrants their first job opportunity.

The Jokerville Slope, or mine, located a short walk west of Crested Butte on Coal Creek, yielded the coal that launched an era of steady production. This mine, opened in September 1881, was the Colorado Coal and Iron's pride, despite an infamous reputation for potentially explosive gas and rock falls. The company received praise in the *Gazette* on October 5, 1883, for its excellent management and infrequency of accidents (coal mining in these days was not known for its safety precautions). Even such an apparently progressive step as the safety lamp was questioned, and dangerous naked-flame lights continued to be used. The new year of 1884 ushered in even more promising times for the Jokerville. Somewhere between 100 and 120 men worked the mine day and night, and heavily loaded trains plowed through snow to carry the coal and coke out of the winter-locked valley. Sometimes it took four engines, paired in front and rear, pushing and pulling, to accomplish the task. If this encouraging start could be maintained, new production records were assured.

Shortly after the day crew entered the mine on a cold January 24, 1884, morning, a thunderous explosion ripped the mine, the shock of which was felt a half mile away. Smoke and gas rolled out the portal; no one needed to be told that a major disaster had taken place. The extent of the catastrophe could not immediately be ascertained, since would-be rescuers dared not rush into the gas-choked, smoke filled, shattered mine.

Eleven men working in the chamber farthest from the explosion struggled to safety amid dust and gas, stumbling over rocks, timbers, broken cars, coal, and corpses. It took less than half an hour, but to lucky John Cashion "the time appeared nearer fifteen hours." Seventeen of his companions were not so fortunate. They, too, tried in vain to reach safety; all fell victim to "bad air" after the explosion tore the air fan to pieces.

Tired night shift miners and panicked residents raced to the mine, formed a rescue party amid the twisted debris of timbers and collapsed buildings, and attempted to enter. Gas drove them back. They regrouped, waited, and tried again at eleven o'clock. By that time, little hope remained of finding the men alive. Miners rushed over from the nearby Anthracite Mine to join in the rescue, only to be forced to wait. Not until the badly damaged fan was repaired could fresh air be pumped into the workings and the grim search be safely started. What rescuers saw as they worked their way inward nearly baffled description, "as if a huge cannon had been exploded." Massive chunks of coal lay about, heaps of rock, twisted equipment, demolished wooden walls, and bodies, fifty-nine in all, when the final tally was made. Nobody survived except a few near the portal. A *Gunnison Review-Press* reporter expressed the anguish and horror:

> *[it was] ascertained that at least sixty were in a second of time ushered into eternity. It is the most fearful disaster entailing a greater loss of life than any accident that has ever occurred in Colorado or for that matter in the western states. (January 24)*

> *[fifty-nine men]hurled into eternity — fathers, brothers, sons — who left their homes but an hour before in robust health, kissing loved ones bidding them good-bye, until they should return after their day's work in the evening. The terrible shock has cast a gloom over their beautiful city, and it will be a long time before they can hope to recover from it. (January 26)*

The return home from the day's work never came. The gloom cast by the disaster hung on for years.

Help from outside the immediate area came quickly to stricken Crested Butte. From Gunnison and beyond came money, food, and other items for the widows and orphans. Most of the victims were single, the only circumstance of the tragedy that somewhat mitigated its effects. When the final accounting came in May, money was apportioned according to the number of children per family, at $65 a head. No dollar amount could compensate for the loss of a husband and father. On the trains into Crested Butte rode the county sheriff, state mine inspector, county commissioners, and Colorado Coal and Iron officials, including the general manager, chief surgeon, and attorney. The company did what it could, erecting a frame building to house the bodies and to hold the funeral services, making ample provisions for the needy families, and bearing all funeral expenses, including sending bodies and families East. Only six of the miners had families living in Crested Butte; each was consoled as much as possible by company officials in what must have been tense, sad visits.

In Colorado's worst mining disaster to date, an unsought record Crested Butte held for years, all the victims were of English origin. In the coal mining annals of Colorado, there has never been, before or since, such ethnic homogeneity. Not all victims were adult men; Tommy Lyle and William Neath, both about twelve, worked as gate keepers, and Morgan Neath, seventeen, was a driver. Nor was it unusual to have more than one member of the same family filled. Fathers took their sons at an early age to work in the mines, first at easier jobs, then as coal miners in a two-man team with themselves.

Crested Butte rallied its support for the sufferers. A benefit show raised some money; more important, friends and neighbors came to offer aid and comfort. The horror of the tragedy became a lasting memory for those who experienced it, young or old. W.C. Cuthbert wrote to the *Elk Mountain Pilot* on May 2, 1940 that he still recalled it. As a lad of five, he remembered the miners digging through the snow at night by the light of little lamps to open the road to the cemetery. Fifty-six years after the explosion the image was fresh in his mind.

The cause of most of the deaths proved fairly easy to determine: those not killed by the blast were overcome by the afterdamp, a mixture of gases, principally "carbonic acid gas and nitrogen." Colorado's new state coal mine inspector carried out his first gruesome investigation, concluding that "causalities seem to be inseparable from the conduct of this business." He went on to point out that the mine had been plagued by firedamp, a flammable explosive gas when mixed with air in certain proportions. Only two months earlier seven miners had been badly burned in a smaller explosion. Easy enough to certify, these facts did not ameliorate the grief nor quiet the mounting anger aimed at Colorado Coal and Iron.

Colonel M.L. De Courcey, described by the *Rocky Mountain News* as a prominent citizen of Crested Butte, provided some interesting opinions in an interview printed January 27. The death of so many miners would prove a great financial loss to the merchants, he solemnly intoned, and the time other miners were kept from working entailed the loss of hundreds of dollars every week. "The worst financial result, however, is that it puts a temporary damper on the camp." Damper, indeed! De Courcey went on to say:

> *Do not know as I ought to say it but I think the company is making one great mistake in not getting all the facts in the matter before the public. It looks as if they were concealing things from the newspaper, and getting press reports fixed up to suit themselves. Do not see how the company [could] have been to blame for the accident, and I do not see why they should make any concealment of facts.*

Sometimes the Victorian American business mind could be extremely one-tracked, even in tragedy.

Greatly shocked, William Palmer responded immediately to news of the disaster by telegraphing $1,000 to be divided among the suffering families and sending in company officials to find out what had happened and why. He was not alone in wondering why.

Identification and burial of the victims became the first order of business. The company did its best by telegraphing "every part of the country," endeavoring to uncover relatives of the dead men. Those remaining unclaimed were buried on January 29 in a mass grave. A town draped in mourning, with flags at half mast, saw the sleighs, each carrying two bodies, depart for the cemetery. About three feet of new snow complicated the final Catholic and Protestant services. Even that fresh white snow, however, could not mask the charred remains back at the mine or the dirt of freshly dug graves.

A coroner's jury was quickly impaneled to conduct hearings. Meanwhile, ugly rumors circulated around the camp. The Mollie Maguires, that infamous Pennsylvania terrorist group that avenged coal miners, reportedly threatened the life of John Gibson, the mine boss. If not the Mollies, other men considered lynching him. Why Gibson? He was blamed for allowing men to work and use exposed lights in that extremely gaseous mine; Gibson became a convenient scapegoat for the company. In addition, some men apparently held old grudges against him and may have wanted to use the accident as a cover to even the score. No real attempt was made to carry out the threats, however.

After hearing the testimony and examining the site, the jury concluded that the explosion occurred in "room 18 of entry no. 2," caused by some person or persons entering the room with a naked light. It recommended that hereafter management require employees to use only safety lamps.

This explanation did not satisfy everyone. The *Gunnison Review-Press* promptly spent several February weeks muckraking the disaster and assessing responsibility, raising some interesting questions, many of which are still unanswered today. The fire boss, whose duty it was to check for gas, reported no gas in the mine, except in room 18. He had previously been fired by the company for neglect of duty and reinstated only a few days before the explosion. Had he neglected his duty again? Did the coroner select jurors friendly to the superintendent and the company? Was the company careless; did it violate state law on mine entries and safety precautions? Were certain miners excluded from testifying at the hearing because they knew too much to suit the company? At least one Crested Butte letter writer cheered the paper:

> *Allow me to congratulate you on the stand you have taken on the side of right and justice in regard to the "Slaughter pen" of the C.C. & I. Co. in this place, hoping that you will continue to give wind to the rottenness of this institution.* (February 11, 1884)

General Manager and Vice President Appleton Danforth presented the official reply and answered the paper's charges on February 9. The company had not violated mining law; indeed, management had gone further than the law required. The state inspector had checked the mine about a month before and found more in the way of safety precautions than he had ever seen in any other mine. Neither the company nor its officers were concealing facts; all they asked was "a fair and candid judgment" by the public, based on a clear statement of fact. The same issue of the paper carried an answer to Danforth. The argument ran on until the public and press finally wearied of it, but it generated little enlightenment and in no way helped to repair the damage done. Fortunately, Crested Butte would never suffer through another accident like it.

The public presentation was one thing, but Danforth wrote Palmer privately on January 31 that he had done everything possible to find out the cause and "set us straight" in the eyes of the law and community. What this meant was that after consultation with superintendent James Robinson and Danforth himself, the Gunnison County coroner, who also happened to be the company's local surgeon at Crested Butte, selected a jury "made up of smart, intelligent businessmen who are well known to be friendly to our company." Danforth felt their position to be very strong, because they had complied with the law and provided safety lamps. The fire boss inspected the whole mine every morning before the miners went in and marked places where gas was found. Room 18 had been so marked. Revealing more than he intended, he went on to mention that the men proved to be more careful when naked lamps were used than after safety lamps had been introduced. The thorough Danforth busied himself writing resolutions expressing local sentiment to show outsiders how people "on the ground looked at the matter." Only "Father Dunna (?)" knew who the author was; Danforth found him "a most valuable assistant" and proposed to Palmer that he be sent $25.

Palmer could have been nothing but pleased with the hard working, painstaking Danforth. In the end, the company weathered the storm. The letter, however, gives a candid insight into company tactics and business morality of the day. Not alone, the Colorado Coal and Iron only mirrored what was happening elsewhere in mining during those years. Accident after accident was blamed publicly on careless miners.

In the aftermath, little else could be done but pick up the pieces and go on. Crested Butte gained some detrimental national publicity, when newspapers carried accounts and three of the leading magazines, *National Police Gazette, Harper's Weekly,* and *Frank Leslie's Weekly,* added illustrations. In normal times publicity was welcomed; towns and businesses thrived on it (though local residents sometimes abhorred the elements that generated it). But coal mining communities understood that coal mining had been and would continue to be dangerous. Editorial comments in Colorado papers summarized it well:

> *It must be borne in mind that an explosion is an incident rather than an accident of the business of coal mining. Explosive gases are constantly escaping from the beds of coal into the chambers, and it is not always possible to prevent ignition and destruction.*
> (*Rocky Mountain News,* January 25, 1884)

> *In mining country these disasters will occur, and it seems that they cannot be avoided. It is so alike in Pennsylvania and in England, and it will doubtless become more so in this state, as the mines are developed and the force of miners is increased.*
> (*Leadville Herald,* January 26, 1884)

Both writers could not have been more correct.

The Colorado Coal and Iron reopened the Jokerville Mine in May, and soon the ovens again belched smoke and D&RG trains carried coke and coal to outside markets. Plans were announced to build a large number of houses for the miners and erect an office in the vicinity of the mine. When mining engineer Charles Rolker examined all the company property that spring, he found it to be a promising operation, containing the "cream of Colorado properties." Of Crested Butte, he reported that the mine had a good deal of gas and water, which he hoped could be eliminated by a new opening. He scolded both the company and the railroad for not following a conciliatory policy toward each other, because, adding to other problems, the two stood at loggerheads over rates and cars.

With the mine back in operation, Crested Butte slowly returned from the valley of the shadow, into which it had plunged in January. A $10,000 payday boosted business. By the end of the year, progress on the new opening was creating renewed interest. Located higher and to the southwest of the original workings, it was above the water level and promised to be less gassy.

Finally abandoned in May 1885, the Jokerville portal was boarded shut, ending the first chapter of Crested Butte coal mining. Nature would reclaim the site; then only men's memories and the graves in the cemeteries would serve as reminders of the disaster — Colorado's biggest to date.

The Colorado Coal and Iron Board of Directors resolved to erect a monument over the Crested Butte graves, but nothing came of the idea. For the rest of the decade no out-of-the-ordinary tragedies befell Crested Butte. Falling rock was the typical reported cause of fatal accidents. In some years, such as 1889, there were no recorded deaths, but accidents continued to plague the industry. If the miner could not be successfully treated by the local company doctor, he was sent to the hospital in Pueblo, where facilities ranked with the best available in the state.

Noted Colorado mining geologist and engineer Arthur Lakes made an inspection of the new mine in 1885, during the course of which he observed some interesting things. The coal seam was free of slate and soft, easily mined with a pick alone; two men could turn out about nine tons daily. No powder was being used and every precaution was being taken, because "a ticking sound is heard constantly from the escape of gases in the coal." The mine, Lakes believed, contained the greatest concentration of dangerous gas in Colorado. Fortunately, the ventilation appeared to be ample at present. He concluded by praising the coke being produced as probably the best in the state, if not in the West.

The second half of the eighties saw Crested Butte prosper. By 1887, a force of 350 men worked at the mine, and the payroll and purchases gave financial support to town residents and local ranchers alike. Someone did, after all, have to furnish feed for the mules that strained to pull the loaded cars down to the portal entrance. To promote itself favorably, the company had exhibited at the National Mining Exposition in Denver, Crested Butte claiming a prominent place among the coal exhibits.

In his 1889-90 report, the state coal inspector noted that, even though the Crested Butte miners used safety lamps exclusively, explosive gas persisted as somewhat of a problem. The

Rocky Mountain News, discussing the company mines in a December 13, 1891, article, noted that the mine produced 100 tons of coal and 225 tons of coke daily, employing about 500 men: Scotch, Irish, Germans, Americans, and Italians. Crested Butte had emerged as the most important of the mountain coal mining districts; coal mining, not hard-rock, was now unquestionably its chief business.

It had gained its status in the coal realm at the expense of the men who labored deep in the dark coal mine day after day. Colorado Fuel and Iron thought of installing electricity as early as 1885 but did not carry out the idea. Working conditions were never good. Men were paid by the ton for coal removed; timbering, loading, and dead work (work that is not directly productive) received no pay. Only the actual digging of coal earned an income; hence, many coal miners worked just the width of the vein, sometimes crawling on hands and knees as it narrowed, timbering only when absolutely necessary for safety. This helps explain the high number of accidents from falling rocks.

It was important to be on good terms with the boss, who directed the miner and his partner to their work area. A spot in a wide vein near the tracks produced more coal per labor hour than an isolated, narrow vein. It was also important to be on the good side of the driver — one who was slow in getting his car back to the work site could severely limit a day's production. Then, last but certainly not least, was the check-weigher, or checkweighman, who weighed the cars and credited each miner for tonnage. A dishonest one could secretly short cars to receive a company kickback. Coal mining took the combination of a diplomat's skill, hard worker's energy, and gambler's boldness to survive.

The pay a miner received varied with the year but was generally higher in the earlier years because of a shortage of miners. Reported to be as high as $1.50 per ton in 1882, $.90 was more likely. By 1886 wages had slipped to an average of $.89 per 2,000-pound ton (this was the short ton; some companies insisted on a 2,200-pound ton, the long ton), and five years later the company averaged $.65 per ton. Some mine owners paid as low as $.50. This decline in wages predictably created tension, leading to a labor crisis in the winter of 1890-91. Coal mining's seasonal nature meant that a strike in the peak production winter months would undermine profits faster than one in July. When the Crested Butte miners demanded a $.10 per ton increase in late November of 1890, the company acquiesced quickly — but not permanently. Officials secretly planned to remove the increase as soon as weather permitted a reduction of shipments to cover the summer trade demands. They had to depress wages when sales slackened in order to justify the lower rate at the beginning of the next winter's trade. As heartless and deceptive as this was, it was good business, and Colorado Coal and Iron knew that good business, not labor, had backboned Colorado.

What kind of men "sold their souls" to work for the company under dangerous, ill-paid conditions? Not skilled, hard-rock miners, who disdained labor in the coal mines. The clearest look at Crested Butte coal miners for this era comes from the 1885 Colorado census, the 1890 original returns for the federal census having been destroyed. The majority of the miners were foreign-born, England, Scotland, Wales. As might be expected, coal-oriented Pennsylvania contributed the most American-born miners. Sixty-two percent were single, understandably; this was not an occupation for married men, as the 1884 accident graphically demonstrated. Insurance companies would not risk policies on such a dangerous occupation, and coal companies did not fill the void, even though they might come to the aid of stricken families after an accident. The miners were young, in their twenties or early thirties, very few in their teens or over fifty. They claimed overwhelmingly to be able to read and/or write; only 19 out of 179 said they were illiterate.

No other occupation came anywhere near being so significant to Crested Butte's economy. By 1890, the highest paid and most skilled miners could earn, at $.65 a ton, up to $108 per month. The less fortunate and less experienced dipped as low as $56. Drivers received $77 per month, common laborers on the surface $57. Coke men earned $58 to $79, depending on their responsibility and skill. For these wages they all labored at the Crested Butte mine, providing a living for themselves and profits for the Colorado Coal and Iron.

Those profits intrigued the investor and justified a multitude of transgressions, if not outright sins. They also interested the Durango Trust, later the Durango Land and Coal, so named because its main investment had gone toward establishing that Colorado town and getting coal mines operating there. Among its other investments were the Crested Butte Town Company and coal lands that were leased to the Colorado Coal and Iron. This created a tidy little arrangement, since some of the same men invested in both. The lease, including the Jokerville, was to run for ninety-nine years, with royalties from $.08 to $.15 per ton on coal and coke. The Trust obviously expected yearly dividends, something that was not always forthcoming. It blamed the Colorado Coal and Iron for not making the most of opportunities, for keeping the price of coke too high, and for cutting timber off the lease without paying the required royalty. In the end, there seemed little it could do except take what was offered and hope for more. These impediments notwithstanding, the Trust's revenue reached $18,894 in the period from 1886 to 1888, far better than the income from the shares of the town company, which yielded nothing and created a burden rather than a profit.

How many of these complaints were actually justified and how many were simply generated by dashed expectations will never be known. However, other individuals also complained about Colorado Coal, largely because of its association with the D&RG. The *Garfield Banner* in nearby Tincup stated, on February 4, 1882, that private parties were unable to secure coal cars while the company got all it needed. Shipping rates were discriminatory, ranging up to a dollar more per ton for individuals than for the company. Company domination brought with it certain facts of business life that Coloradans were just beginning to grasp.

One of the great expectations of the Durango Trust centered on anthracite and the Anthracite Mesa Coal Mining Company, in which it owned 633 shares. Almost from the start, Crested Butte had been known for its anthracite deposits, though the nearest important ones were five miles northwest of the camp at Smith Hill, also known as Anthracite, and beyond at Irwin. Until Crested Butte emerged on the scene, Pennsylvania anthracite stood unchallenged; now, for the first time, a western field had been opened.

Howard Smith shipped the first large quantity of anthracite in early 1882 to Pueblo, Denver, and other points along the D&RG line, but the reception proved lukewarm, "owing to want of sufficient preparation." Undiscouraged, the Anthracite Mesa Coal Company spent a busy 1882 erecting a tramway from railroad track to mine, an impressive coal breaker (with screens to clean the anthracite and for separating six different lump sizes of coal), a boarding house, and a store. By the end of the year other buildings contributed to the improved appearance of a young and budding community.

The year 1883 was notable for the tragic snow slide that struck the recently completed boarding house, killing seven men and injuring fourteen more. Nature maintained its influence over mining and miners. Anthracite mining was somewhat different from bituminous. The mine cars were larger, with a 2½ to 3 ton capacity on the average, and the coal often contained seams of slate frequently impossible to separate while mining, hence the need for the breaker to separate slate and other refuse. This requirement probably undermined Smith's early selling and shipping venture. In addition, the coal by its very nature had to have a uniform draft to burn; this could be accomplished only through separation of anthracite into grades of uniform size, the other breaker function.

Anthracite Mesa Coal, under the presidency of Palmer's good friend William Bell (also director of the Durango Trust), could proudly point to the fact that it had the only breaker west of Pennsylvania and 100 employees, twenty-five at the mill and seventy-five in the mine. Its production lagged behind Crested Butte through those years. Located slightly farther up the mountains, along a steep hillside, the anthracite mine was more vulnerable to the heavy winter snowfalls and dangerous snow slides, which often curtailed work. Mining, transportation, marketing, and the weather finally proved too much for the original owners of Anthracite Mesa, and in August 1884 they leased the mine and breaker to the year-old Denver-based Colorado Fuel Company, presenting Colorado Coal with a rival for dominance of all the major mines. In December of that year, Uncle Sam recognized the mine's importance and established a post office at the breaker, appropriately named Anthracite.

Colorado Fuel enthusiastically set about mining its five-foot seam of anthracite. By 1887, 400 tons went to the United States mint in San Francisco, but the bulk of anthracite shipments went to Denver and Salt Lake City. Aggressive John C. Osgood and his Colorado Fuel Company did more than simply move in on the older Colorado Coal in Crested Butte. They challenged it across the state, threatening the financial stability of both. As a result, the two finally and logically merged in October 1892, to become Colorado Fuel and Iron Company. One company now controlled all the major mines; after twelve years, Crested Butte would feel the full force of corporation control.

Before that happened, however, Colorado Coal and Iron became entangled in a messy strike related to wages — it was long overdue. When an 1884 strike hit the company, the mountain district remained unaffected, Crested Butte miners hardly being in a position to strike that year. As mentioned before, the threat of a strike in 1890 brought some wage relief, though not for long: the company planned to reduce wages. However, Pandora's box was opened by a different problem. Dissatisfaction with the mine superintendent reportedly lay at the root of the trouble, probably because he symbolized the company at the local level. When violence erupted in early March of 1891, Gunnison County Sheriff Cyrus "Doc" Shores arrived to arrest the leaders of the "riot." Some workers who ignored the strike were apparently beaten "unmercifully" while walking home, spurring citizens to telegraph for help.

With the arrest and trial of the leaders (two found guilty of disturbing the peace), the situation calmed temporarily. A new wrinkle, ethnic prejudice, was introduced in the newspaper coverage. "Hungarians are not wanted in this country." American labor, claimed the *Gunnison Tribune*, would have settled the differences peaceably. The paper, however, also castigated the company: "This county cannot afford to bear the burden of strikes. The C.C.&I. Co. should protect its own property." Lake City's *Hinsdale Phonograph* also evidenced irritation because the strike threatened local mines dependent upon coal; it advocated a state law to prevent work stoppages. Just to be fair, the editor went to the other extreme and advocated a law to protect employees from "oppression and abuse" by employers who have no care "but to increase profits as much as possible." Neither proposal had even a long shot chance of passing, and Colorado Coal paid little attention to these mutterings.

Simmering resentment against Colorado Coal and Iron management and policies flared up again in November when employees were notified that on December 1 wages would be reduced by $.10 per ton, to $.65 per ton, for miners, and for day laborers on a corresponding scale. Their ready answer was a strike.

Everything was peaceful at first. Each side held firm; a week passed, with neither giving an inch. Attitudes hardened; both sides grew tense. The increasingly desperate miners did not have the resources to maintain a prolonged strike, and they struck on their own; no union or outside agency came to their aid. The company was losing business at its peak season, losses that quickly translated into deficits in the ledger book.

"RIOTING!" screamed an inflammatory headline in the *Rocky Mountain News* on December 12, 1891. Five men were killed, the article claimed, when the coal miners took possession of the mine; Italian miners stirred up the trouble and created the riot; the town was alarmed and armed; and the county sheriff and a posse were hurrying to the rescue. The *News's* readers received an account reinforcing the current image of coal miners and strikers — foreign agitators who resorted to violence.

Calmer reflection showed that what had occurred should have been expected. The majority of the miners were Austrians and Italians; a company policy encouraged the hiring of these recently docked immigrants. Unused to American ways and with no organization, they struck. Unfortunately, agitators gained a hearing as the strike dragged on, resulting in a miners' parade on Friday, the eleventh. With a brass band and American flag leading, the procession appeared harmless enough. On the other hand, miners "armed to the teeth" seemed threatening. Alarmed citizens, including the mayor, John Tetard, wired to Gunnison for Sheriff Shores. The sheriff and an armed posse arrived that evening near midnight, the train proceeding directly to the mine to disembark its passengers. Hearing of the train's arrival, strikers rushed to meet it, assuming it to be a trainload of scabs. Someone fired a gun, and a barrage of shots broke the night tension, sending miners running back to Crested Butte and leaving the posse holding the mine property under a quickly established siege. Seven miners were wounded in the skirmish.

The wildest rumors circulated in the community and alarmed the entire state. Numbers wounded or killed, intentions of both sides (violent), and the possibility of peaceful settlement (slim) changed with each telling. Mayor Tetard and mine superintendent William Grant were warned to leave or be killed. The sheriff threatened to shoot anyone who crossed his self-imposed "dead line" at the foot of the hill. Not shrinking from the fight, the miners threatened to blow up the mine portal and buildings. Nervous businessmen hired guards to protect the waterworks, fearing an attempt to burn the town, and both the Congregationalists and the Catholics heard Sunday sermons urging men to avoid conflict.

Governor John Routt, fearing the conflict might become as violent as predicted, sent the Deputy State Commissioner of Labor, Lester Bodine, to mediate the dispute. The company rushed in its general manager, E.M. Steck, and general superintendent, George Ramsey. Steck managed to dispatch a series of agitative telegrams, which did nothing but add fuel to the fire. Bodine was in for a hard time, if the company's statement that the miners go back to work or the mine would be shut down indefinitely meant anything. The strikers selected spokesmen and discussions began. Representatives of the company, miners, local businessmen, and Bodine met at the Elk Mountain Hotel. The miners claimed they could not make living wages on $.65 per ton and mentioned a few other grievances, including scarcity of cars for loading coal and having to carry props too far, thereby losing work time. Colorado Coal logically pointed out $.65 had been the wage for years, and they could not maintain operations at $.75 because of competition. Both sides blamed the other for starting the violence; the miners feared that the train brought strike breakers, the sheriff feared for his life.

In Denver, the *News*, calmed somewhat, showed sympathy for the miners' plight in a bold editorial:

Of course, as society is now organized, they should either work for whatever wages, however beggarly they be, their employers are willing to pay, or peacefully give up their places; but if they don't, let them not be judged too harshly. (December 14, 1891)

The owners were at fault, the paper went on; men could not be expected to watch their families starve because their wages were too low. "The great company seeks to cut wages" when the wages being paid "are only enough to keep soul and body together" and provide a hovel called home. Those were strong words, but it remained to be seen what effect they might have.

The first hearings resulted only in continued deadlock, Shores holding the property, and the miners, not knowing quite what to do, gathering in little groups to watch and talk. What this did was buy time, allowing passions to cool and rumors to be checked out. Bodine telegraphed Routt on the thirteenth: "All quiet. I addressed 200 miners and told them to keep the peace, pending my arrangement for an amicable settlement. They have complied. No one killed. Previous reports exaggerated." That was it in a nutshell.

Bodine finally got the company to put a proposition on the table, offering to remedy the grievances and return to the old schedule as soon as prices permitted. That did not satisfy the miners' spokesmen, who pointed out the higher cost of living at Crested Butte than at other camps, such as El Moro. Neither did it seem fair to reduce the number of miners in order to insure more cars for their use. They did take the offer to the miners' meeting where, as expected, it was rejected. Bodine tried to find a compromise and failed.

Fortunately for Crested Butte, no new violence disturbed the armed truce, although threats against the foreigners caused new complications. Fearing an outbreak of anti-Italian violence (Italian miners were being blamed for the shooting), the Italian Consul in Denver, Frank Bruni Grimaldi, accused Hungarians and Austrians of leading his countrymen astray and telegraphed them:

To the Italian miners of Crested Butte: I exhort you for your interest in the Italian name and country to let yourself be drawn aside: to cease resisting and trust to the equity and justice of Americans and to wait.

What they would gain by waiting was unclear; time was against them. The company's ploy became clear now. General Agent George Cook clearly presented it when he commented that miners were ready to go to work, but they were being threatened by the Austrians, Hungarians, and Italians. Time allied itself with Colorado Coal, which did not have to work for room and board. With Christmas approaching, the married miner faced a terrible dilemma.

Further meetings brought no concessions from either side, and Bodine left for Denver on the sixteenth. His mission failed only in the sense that a compromise had not been reached. The meetings provided a discussion forum, defusing the aftermath of the shooting.

That same day the miners' solid front showed signs of collapsing when, during their meeting, some men moved to allow strikers to load the coke ready to be shipped. They simply wanted to earn money to live on. Amid great excitement, the motion was declared out of order. It was only a matter of hours now. Steck (whom the *News* described as "hot headed"), reportedly very bitter against the Italians, now hinted that they would not be taken back under any circumstances. He, Shores, and armed deputies advanced to the coke ovens on the seventeenth, a prearranged signal to a group of Austrians to come out of their houses and go to work loading coke into cars. The sheriff also posted deputies at convenient places throughout town, apparently to intimidate anyone who thought of causing any further trouble.

After a few more rumors, three mysterious skyrockets shot from an Italian house, and a "night of terror" highlighted by a meeting of Italian strikers, it was announced that the mine would open on the nineteenth. Knowing it was over, Steck returned to Denver, where he praised the company for its conservative handling of the strike and blamed the Italians for taking the lead in causing trouble.

The strike was finished — the miners had lost. Although they had vocal support from the Denver Trades' Assembly, they fought alone. The company remained too strong, and its policy of divide and conquer worked to perfection. A *Denver Republican* reporter on the scene reported on the sixteenth that men of different nationalities were not mingling by that time, and that the English-speaking people were joining the Austrians against the Italians.

On the eighteenth, Shores and his deputies moved to arrest those deemed guilty; only taunts and jeers greeted them as they stalked the streets. Among those arrested were Jim Barto, "a swarthy looking Italian," John Follette, an Italian saloon keeper, and Austrian Joe Papish, all accused of being ringleaders. Others were seized, but charges against them were dismissed. The newspapers created infinite variations in their attempts to spell the unfamiliar names. No Italians needed to reapply for work — they were automatically refused employment. In groups and individually they left Crested Butte. The American dream had temporarily been dashed for them.

Now came the strike's aftermath with its charges and countercharges of blame, the company receiving the worst of it. Editorial comments from near and far blasted them:

Colorado Coal and Iron deservedly is receiving the greatest censure from the state press. Well it may be for the contemptible parts its representatives have taken in this matter.
(Gunnison Tribune, December 26, 1891)

When will the laboring man learn that Capital is King, and can, at will, control all the machinery of the law?
(White Pine Cone, December 25, 1891)

Their object has been to get not only cheap labor, but ignorant labor — their philosophy being that cheapness and ignorance in labor naturally went hand in hand. The result has been that to force the mining of coal to the lowest possible figure, intelligent labor has been squeezed out and their places filled with Italian, Huns, Slavs. These poor, ignorant foreigners at Crested Butte are not criminals in fact or by nature. Their labor is the most slavish in the country.
(Rocky Mountain News, December 14, 1891)

Steck earned the sharpest criticism. The Denver Trades' Assembly charged him with trapping the miners' delegation into conspiracy statements during the meetings, a charge Bodine supported. Steck returned the blast, accusing Bodine of favoring the miners. Then the war of words died down, along with general public interest in Crested Butte. Colorado Coal and Iron remained firmly enthroned — to the victors belonged the spoils.

The community returned to normal after the start of the new year. No longer did businessmen pay guards to protect the waterworks and fire apparatus; neither did deputies patrol the streets nor ministers preach sermons about labor violence. The strike was history; 230 miners had walked out — 70 Italians, 130 Austrians, and 30 English-speaking men — but had accomplished little. The charges against the three leaders still held in Gunnison were dismissed in March.

During the twelve years just past, Crested Butte had moved through a somewhat typical scenario for an American coal mining district and community of this era. The tragic explosion and strike were common occurrences, unfortunately; so was the introduction of foreign miners to replace Americans and British. Nor were the attitudes of Colorado Coal and Iron out of line with its contemporaries; business reigned triumphant at that time. The significance of the railroad to economic growth and prosperity paralleled what happened elsewhere.

That Crested Butte did not become solely a company town does not fit the pattern. Starting as a hard-rock camp, it never evolved into a true company town, completely controlled by one corporation. The setting did not remind one of a coal camp — it was too beautiful in its mountain-surrounded valley. The stereotyped drabness of company housing, huddled on a desolate site against a backdrop of mine buildings, did not hold true here.

What the future held in store was unknown in 1892. If it proved anything like the past decade it promised to be exciting, but, it was hoped, not so tragic. The newly organized Colorado Fuel and Iron would have to wait and see.

Crested Butte, 1880-1900:
A PHOTOGRAPHIC ESSAY

Henry Ford once declared there was "no such thing as no chance" in the land of opportunity called America; Crested Butte exemplified the ideal in the first twenty years of its existence. From trail-breaking pioneers to turn-of-the-century immigrants, the community and its mines offered that hope, that expectation. Why else would these people have come to work and live in the valley of the Elk Mountains? There certainly were much more agreeable places to take up habitation.

The photographs that follow permit a glimpse of a life that is long gone from Colorado. Consider carefully what is displayed — a hard-rock camp that evolves into a coal town is a rarity, highly unusual in Colorado's history.

Crested Butte in the winter of 1895 showed signs of prosperity and had a population approaching 1,000. From this distance, it looked much like its hard-rock neighbors, and its community aspirations were much the same.
Denver Public Library, Western History Department

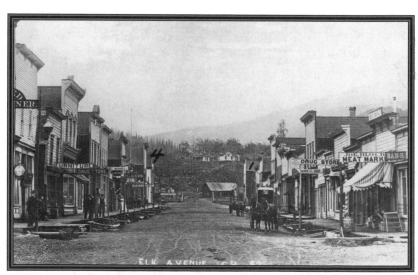

Elk Avenue, Crested Butte's business heart, offers a variety of stores to tempt the customer on this rather lazy summer afternoon. False-fronted wooden construction was typical of nineteenth-century mining camps, as were advertising signs straddling the sidewalk.
Denver Public Library, Western History Department

In January 1890, and again three years later, Crested Butte's business district suffered devastating fires. Both times winter weather hampered the "fire laddies" and, as this January 1893 photo shows, the fire itself and the dynamiting to create fire breaks caused widespread destruction.

Denver Public Library, Western History Department

When Joseph Block (white apron) posed before his meat market, a handful of youngsters, friends, and a passerby joined him. One-time Denver, Black Hawk, and Central City butcher, Colorado pioneer Block came to Irwin in '80 before moving to Crested Butte.

Denver Public Library, Western History Department

The Elk Mountain Pilot started in Irwin then migrated to Crested Butte in 1884, where it was published until mid-1949. It provided a major source of information on local life and times.

Colorado Historical Society

John W. Rockefeller (left) was a long-time Crested Butte doctor and businessman. This enterprising physician involved himself in banking and the electric company.

Denver Public Library, Western History Department

Horace Tabor underwrote the establishment of Crested Butte's bank as part of his financial empire. During a long and varied career, it contributed to making the town a banking and business center.
Duane Vandenbusche

Until the 1890s Crested Butte did not have a company store, that infamous institution of coal mining communities. Then the Colorado Supply Company store appeared, a hand-maiden of the Colorado Fuel and Iron Company.
Denver Public Library, Western History Department

Despite high hopes for silver, Crested Butte's future rested on the black bedrock of coal. The Jokerville Mine produced steadily, and miners gambled their lives in its unsafe, gassy depths. Fifty-nine miners lost the gamble on January 24, 1884; the aftermath of the tragedy is shown here.

Colorado Historical Society

The Jokerville disaster produced undesirable national attention. These drawings appeared in Harper's Weekly.

Harper's Weekly, February 16, 1884

The Big Mine, opened in 1894, proved to be Crested Butte's longest lived and most productive. To the left stand the coke ovens and homes of some of the miners.

Colorado Historical Society

Hot, hard, sooty, and dirty work at the coke ovens gave immigrants a chance to make a start. The next step up was work in the mines.

Denver Public Library, Western History Department

Without lumbering, coal mining would have been hard pressed to maintain itself at Crested Butte. Two lumber wagons stop momentarily on Elk Avenue, bringing logs that will probably be used to timber the Big Mine.

Denver Public Library, Western History Department

Crested Butte's hose team looks sharp on July 4, 1896. If water was available and the weather not too adverse, they stood a chance against the scourge of Colorado mountain towns — fire. Unfortunately, the odds usually were against them.

Denver Public Library, Western History Department

When Joseph Block went home from work, he ended up here, a typical frame house. It was 1890 and Block (#4), wife Louise (#3), and several family members and friends joined for a portrait. The Blocks came from France and Switzerland.

Denver Public Library, Western History Department

Neither of these lads looks too happy about having to pull the lady; maybe they just did not want their pictures taken in such attire. The residential part of Elk Avenue and the tower of Rock School form the background.

Denver Public Library, Western History Department

Winter could be fun at Crested Butte, especially for youngsters. Rock School, the community's pride, sits in the background; built in 1883, it replaced earlier frame structures.
Denver Public Library, Western History Department

A tribute to America's Independence Day, 1898 version, with impressively decorated carriages. The patriotic riders, Ernestine Block and Alberta Metzler, represented two of Crested Butte's leading merchant families.
Denver Public Library, Western History Department

CHAPTER 3
CF&I Assumes Control
1892-1914

A new era began — Colorado Fuel and Iron now guided Crested Butte's present and future. This simple statement belies the tremendously significant impact of the company's influence. With a stronger financial base and larger mining/industrial empire than its predecessor, CF&I not only wielded its might here, but also throughout Colorado. For instance, the *Engineering and Mining Journal*, December 29, 1906, estimated that ten percent of Colorado's wage earners were dependent upon CF&I. In Crested Butte it operated the major mine, had by far the largest payroll, and controlled or leased other coal properties. The independence of the earlier days eroded steadily until it was only a savored memory.

CF&I had come with plans to make a profit, and it fulfilled those plans in the decades ahead. Its first move was to phase out the mine that had been opened after the Jokerville tragedy, at the same time digging a new drift. These things happened quickly, and the famous Big Mine started its operation in 1894 on the mesa directly south of town, with a predicted ("guaranteed," according to the company) fifty-year coal reserve. The older mine was abandoned in December 1895. for the rest of Crested Butte's coal mining era, the well-named Big Mine would be CF&I's principal local operation.

The Durango Land and Coal (the renamed Trust), which still leased land to what was now CF&I, attributed the abandonment partly to the Evans lawsuit. This troublesome, time-consuming, and, worst of all, costly case had to be resolved before the company could hope to consolidate its holdings and achieve that cherished profit.

The case grew out of a tangled question of land ownership that reverted to the time the Utes controlled the region. That in itself would not have been serious if 80 of the disputed 160 acres had not included the "main entry, air courses and numerous cross entries" of the mine. Briefly, the history was this. Roger Evans filed on coal land in 1880, only to have the Land Office suspend final purchase because a portion of it lay on the Ute Reservation. A year later, while Evans still had rights, along came Byron McMaster, who filed on the same land for the Durango Trust. He neither notified Evans nor fully complied with land office requirements. Meanwhile, the land was leased to the Colorado Coal and Iron, which commenced mining. Everything went along smoothly until 1891, when the government notified Evans to appear and show cause why his original entry should not be canceled. After consulting his lawyer, Evans sued, seeking "plunder," according to the disgruntled Durango Land and Coal group, but, according to him, seeking $1.4 million in damages for coal mined. The case dragged on for six years, clouding ownership and stalling work. Although Evans never gained control of the actual operations, the threat that he might always lurked on the horizon, hence the switch to the Big Mine. Neither side had a particularly strong case. Evans, however, presented the better argument. A worried CF&I finally decided to settle out of court in September 1898.

The settlement involved $7,000 for Evans and $16,500 for his two lawyers, who ended up owning part of his claim. With that matter out of the way, CF&I could breathe more easily, and the Durango Land and Coal could receive its royalties. Thanks to the skill of CF&I lawyers and the weakness of Evans's claim, the result proved less costly than anticipated. This case illustrated, here as elsewhere in the West, the nature of the legal entanglements that could embroil a successful mine because of unclear, faulty, or downright fraudulent filing of the original claims. CF&I was no stranger to this type of litigation.

CF&I set about its business in earnest. Its Crested Butte operation, the largest of its mountain mines, was the only one producing anthracite. Anthracite, of course, did not come from the Big Mine. The Smith Hill Mine continued to produce anthracite, though only spasmodically after 1900 (CF&I finally gave up its lease in 1907). The major effort went into opening what became known as Floresta, some eleven miles west of Crested Butte, where coal had once been mined for the nearby Ruby/Irwin mines. In 1893 the D&RG built an extension to this isolated, 10,000-foot mine and its neighboring hamlet. Heavy snowfalls, huge drifts, and long winters smothered all efforts from the start. So did the thin, three-foot, steeply angled coal seam, which made it impossible for any but the most experienced miners to earn an acceptable wage based upon daily tonnage, even when digging high grade anthracite. Married men could not risk moving there because of the unpredictable, usually short mining season, and most single men were not enchanted with the prospects either. A hundred or so miners made up the crew, and Floresta limped along, the only redeeming factor being its rare anthracite coal. As a bituminous operation, it would have sunk into oblivion.

Bituminous coal continued to be the backbone of Crested Butte. Production mounted steadily at the Big Mine until it was being called by the *Denver Times*, in its January 1899 New Year's edition, one of the largest coal mines in the state, with 21,000 tons of coal and 6,000 tons of coke produced monthly. A year later production set a single month's record of 25,836 and 8,403 tons of coal and coke, respectively, not bad by any standards and exceptional for a mountain coal district. The years from 1897 to 1903 set unsurpassed records. Although work continued to be seasonal, as in the past, it was not shut down by strikes or accidents during these years, an enviable record for such times of general labor unrest and repeated coal mining accidents throughout Colorado.

CF&I strove for efficiency and took pride in the fact that Crested Butte coal did not need washing, a requirement of most other mines producing coking coal. Furthermore, delivery of the coal from mine to consumer entailed only one handling, whether coke or coal was involved. Coal from the dark mine depths went directly to ovens or coal car. The *Elk Mountain Pilot*, November

30, 1911, proudly proclaimed: "mention of its name [Crested Butte] anywhere in the west is a sufficient guarantee of its quality and the demand is constantly increasing as the knowledge of its superiority becomes known by those using it." Demand was accelerated by the opening of a smelter in Salida in 1902, which relied primarily on Crested Butte coal and coke. Coal with low sulfur and ash content always ranked at the top of preferred metallurgical fuels.

The company also basked proudly in the Big Mine's reputation for safety. The state coal mine inspector praised CF&I in 1896 for a two-year record of no fatal accidents at Crested Butte. In the years following 1900 while Colorado coal mining was developing into big business, the industry gained an unenviable reputation for mining accidents, but never the Big Mine, which went from 1905 through 1914 with only four fatal accidents. Compare that to 1910, the year the Jokerville total was surpassed, when explosions killed 75, 56, and 79 coal miners in three separate Colorado mining disasters. Accidents did happen, of course, and a miner was occasionally killed, such as twenty-three-year-old Austrian Joe Dorsey, who was crushed by a rock slab in May 1899. In October 1901, a fellow Austrian, Steve Roziman, was suffocated by gas. CF&I could console itself, if so inclined, by taking to heart the Colorado coal inspector's 1900 comment that "gross" carelessness of miners caused thirty percent of the fatalities, a percentage the company might have been willing to argue was much higher.

CF&I, to its credit, did take precautions to prevent catastrophes. Two miles of water pipe sprinkled the coal dust to keep it down thus, hopefully, preventing an explosion, and any miner who disregarded rules relating to lighted pipes and carrying matches in the mine would be "immediately discharged." Strict discipline was the rule. Even in the best regulated mines, danger prevailed, and everyone received a good scare on Sunday, August 3, 1905, when flames engulfed the compressor room. Four hours later the fire was out, but not before the boiler house, carpenter shop, lamp cabin, 200 feet of snowsheds, and one engine house were smoldering ashes. Until repairs were made, the mine remained closed.

As mentioned, CF&I totally dominated Crested Butte coal mining. As the century turned, its officers became somewhat more aware of their corporate image and were more careful to keep their best face forward. One easy way was to publicize payday by mentioning in the newspaper how much good all those wages did for the community. Another was to praise any new mining development, such as the new tipple in 1912 to better load the trains, which allowed a larger coal output than ever before in the history of the mine. The tipple was planned to accommodate broad-gauge railroad cars for which CF&I, as well as the general population, yearned mightily. That accomplishment would be the frosting on the transportation cake and put a stop to the costly rehandling of Crested Butte coal from narrow to broad-gauge cars. CF&I and D&RG hints never brought the promised "hummer" growth.

Before one begins to think of CF&I's Crested Butte posture as being benevolent and benign beyond belief for those times, one should look to other aspects of its local operation. Profit was still the rule, and safety precautions, improvements, increased production, and broad-gauge connections were all designed to produce it. Mining unions thwarted that goal and were viewed by the company as un-American, a fly in the free enterprise ointment.

The miners, of course, vehemently disagreed. In the unfair contest between the worker and management, they needed all the help they could muster, and union affiliation seemed, at least, to make the struggle less one sided. CF&I heartily opposed miners' organizing and unions — all they could see were strikes, agitation, and increased costs. The factors that motivated the miners to take such action seemed not to concern management very much. It all boiled down to mutual misunderstandings and mounting bitterness, as the strike of 1894 amply demonstrated.

Crested Butte neither initiated or played a major role in this confrontation, which began in April in CF&I's Fremont County coal camps. Miners complained about irregular pay and pay in the form of scrip, which could be exchanged only for face value at company stores. They demanded union recognition. As soon as the strike started, CF&I retaliated by shutting down steel works, mines, and coke ovens. The Crested Butte miners joined the general strike in early May, according to the *Gunnison Tribune* of May 12. However, the *Lake City Times* of June 14 reported that after two meetings the miners decided not to strike, causing bitterness between those who wanted to and those who did not. Regrettably, the Crested Butte papers are missing for this period.

Eighteen-ninety-four was a bad year, the second of the shocking 1890s nationwide depression. A bitter labor dispute at Cripple Creek, Eugene Debs's leading his union members out against the Pullman Company near Chicago, and the Pennsylvania coal field strikes clearly showed the desperation of the times and of the working man. As a result, Crested Butte's threat of a strike did not garner much attention. But the strike did occur, without doubt, because in late July the miners voted to return to work. The town woke up to the "old familiar sound" of the mine whistle, even though the "measly" thing did not work to perfection after weeks of silence.

Elsewhere the strike slowly came to an end without a victory for the miners. This round belonged to CF&I, not unexpectedly. Over in Lake City, the editor of the *Times* (June 28) found a now familiar cause for all this agitation: the "lowest class of imported foreign labor." American-born miners served to maintain the peace he claimed. The obvious lesson, then, was to stop the wholesale importation of foreigners, who were unfit for "self government" in a free country. CF&I, at such times, must have questioned its policy of using foreign miners, many fresh from the old country. But when the threat was weighed against profits, the scales always tipped to the latter.

The scales also tipped heavily against unionization. There would be none of that in CF&I territory. How it handled the situation was demonstrated in 1899. Organizers for the Western Federation of Miners moved into Crested Butte to try to organize a local union. They succeeded in signing some miners before CF&I found out about their efforts. Swiftly came the retaliation — forty men were fired and the mine was closed. Vice President Julian Kebler wrote the Durango Land and Coal that closing the mine was the only thing to do, as "we thought it the best way" to prevent further trouble and a threatened strike. With this procedure the loss would be less, he consoled the Land and Coal people, who possibly doubted the wisdom of such a course of action. In closing Kebler admonished, "I trust that you will keep this quiet, as the reason we gave for shutting the mine down is the heavy expense of the coal, and we do not care to have anyone know the reason."

The men were not fooled in the least and told the representative of the Colorado Bureau of Labor that union organization was the real cause of the shutdown. Although they spoke the truth, the mine and coke ovens stayed closed from May to early July. The town and the entire district suffered, while CF&I cut the union men off its payroll. The Western Federation, more a hard rock than a coal miners' union, did not last long. It was different with the United Mine Workers of America, which appeared around the turn of the century, it was a coal miners union. Its inception, though, proved no more acceptable; organizers were arrested on fictitious charges, driven from coal camps, and its members were blacklisted.

Not wishing to join in a late 1903 strike, Crested Butte miners continued to work. Threats from "outside strike agitators" caused a group of concerned citizens to ask the town's board of trustees for a special meeting to support the local miners. The *Pilot* heartily bolstered the no-strike plan and opposed the United Mine Workers. The Big Mine remained open.

Undaunted, the organizers persisted. By 1908 a peace of sorts had come to Crested Butte, when the *Pilot* (January 2, 1908) could announce that the UMW gave a "Masque Ball" at the Croatian Hall. Maybe the members had to be masked, though that seems doubtful. It was not a peace built on understanding and equality. Attitudes toward miners had not really changed, despite some superficial progress, nor had wages or working conditions improved. Miners too often were thought of as so many machines that could be replaced easily and cheaply. A mule cost more and, in some cases, was better treated. Such attitudes augured ill for the future.

During this time, Crested Butte and its mountain and western neighbors held steady in their role as poor country cousins to the great northern and southern Colorado coal fields, where the mines of Erie and Trinidad out-produced them handily. The situation in those fields generally charted the course of management and labor relations throughout the state after 1900. The long, vicious strikes sparked there and the attitudes generated poisoned the entire industry. Crested Butte might have its own form of peace, but none permeated the districts in the eastern United States. The old issues — unionism, pay, working conditions, nearly feudal control over the workers and their families —

would not die. In one respect, Crested Butte stood like a haven in the storm: it was not a company-developed, controlled, governed, and maintained community as were Cokedale, Berwind, Hastings, and so many others.

CF&I's position in Crested Butte could well allow it to give the union at least the semblance of organization; the real substance of power lay with the company. A needed wage "readjustment" downward created no fears for CF&I. A company official wrote the *Gunnison News Champion*, February 21, 1908, "We do not expect any trouble with our employees, much less a strike. There are too many men who want their jobs." Times were a little hard just then, but such corporation arrogance (perhaps honesty) was unusual. The spokesman went on to say, "In Los Angeles there are a thousand men who would be glad to be called here at any time." Luckily for the company, no one called that bluff. From Los Angeles to Crested Butte in February would have been a climatic shock to the determination of even the most desperate job seeker. Walking the streets in the City of Angels would have seemed like heaven in comparison.

A conflict that had smoldered and burned for two decades flared into a final conflagration in the winter of 1913-14, ending in another tragedy. This time it was at a place called Ludlow, distant from Crested Butte only in the miles that separated them. The causes, reactions, and strike pattern were the same. The miners, backed by the UMW, marched out, demanding union recognition, higher wages, checkweighmen elected by the men, and less CF&I dominance. The company used spies to ferret out union members, then promptly blacklisted them. Management refused to deal with the union, rejected its demands, and responded by closing the mines, forcing the workers and their families out of the company-owned homes. Armed guards marched in to protect company property. The strikers trudged to tent camps, one of which was established at the small railroad siding called Ludlow in Las Animas County. They armed themselves, and the two sides settled in for a long, bitter fight. State militia moved in to provide some semblance of order.

Crested Butte remained on the sidelines in the beginning. Finally, on Monday, October 20, Crested Butte and Floresta miners walked out, closing both mines, which stayed shut for the winter. The local union officials demanded a ten percent advance in wages, full pay for all "dead work," and union recognition. CF&I promptly replied that the men should have asked for a conference, claiming that a satisfactory adjustment "undoubtedly" could have been made. That adjustment would not have included union recognition, which was "out of the question." Calm prevailed at first; the unemployed miners were content to enjoy the fine fall weather. As the days grew colder and shorter, tempers grew hotter, and the strike dragged on with no end in sight. The United Mine Workers sent organizers and officials around to the camps to maintain morale and retain a unified front. Unions sent money in for children whose fathers were on strike. James Jordon visited Crested Butte on several occasions, rallying the troops and discussing the situation. Crested Butte held firm.

The *Pilot* published little news on the strike as it ground on, keeping it all very low key. Perhaps the editor figured that to be the wisest course, or perhaps there was no need to report what was already known. The company may have wished to play down the strike and applied pressure to guarantee that it was. For whatever reason, Crested Butte never moved onto center stage.

At Ludlow, on a spring-like April morning in 1914, the tension was broken with gunfire. National guardsmen and strikers tangled, and when the skirmish was finished the tent colony lay in smoldering ruins. Before the day ended, nineteen people were dead, including thirteen women and children. The "Ludlow Massacre" had become an infamous part of Colorado history. Violence begat violence, and for ten days anarchy reigned in the southern fields around Trinidad and Walsenburg, until United States troops arrived to replace the battered Colorado militia. What had just occurred sent reverberations that have echoed down through the decades. It put the state in a very bad light and closed ten years of labor wars in the mine fields.

Crested Butte's calm was not disturbed, the board of trustees going so far as to notify Governor Elias Ammons that "it is the opinion of the board of trustees that troops are not needed here under present conditions." In early June, state investigators came to gather information, which both sides freely offered. The aftermath of the strike went on until November, when the community and its mines finally returned to more normal circumstances.

Well away from the area of physical destruction, Crested Butte escaped unscathed, at least on the surface. Loss of wages, business, and profits were another matter — both the people and CF&I suffered. For more than a year, there were only a few smaller mines operating in this depressed district. Bitterness and individual hardships were hard to weigh, but the aftereffects of the acrimony lingered for years. Colorado miners, principally from the southern and northern districts, not Crested Butte, drew national attention for their plight and their crusade. CF&I lost more than profits. Under post-Ludlow scrutiny, its tactics and policies were revealed to a shocked public, who learned what it meant to have the company as a partner in one's life. As a result, CF&I backed off from some of their oppressive practices and thereafter found its power curbed. The United Mine Workers lost out entirely, except that they called attention to their members' plight. Union recognition did not come, and several decades would pass before the UMW was resurrected. Neither side could crow over its victories losing more than it gained from this strike. The *Pilot*, on October 8, 1914, went so far as to claim that the long-sought standard gauge connection was a victim of it as well.

The miners had been the ones to fight this battle out in the trenches, so to speak, during the long winter of 1913-14. The company was impersonal; the stockholders who backed it undoubtedly subsisted quite well without those dividends. Without their pay, the miners were reduced to poverty. They put their work and their lives on the line in the long struggle with the CF&I. Exactly who were these tenacious miners, and what were their lives like?

The first question is easier to answer. To reiterate quickly, American, English, and northern European miners dominated back in 1885. By the 1900 census, Austrian miners had moved far out in front (62 percent), followed by Scots (8 percent), Italian (8 percent), and Americans from all sections of the country (8 percent). A more graphic picture of CF&I recruiting policies could not be drawn — there had been a complete turnabout in the composition of Crested Butte's mining crew.

Single miners still outnumbered their married co-workers (57 percent to 43 percent); most of the married miners accepted the risk inherent to the job. Crested Butte, however, had always attracted a high percentage of married miners, compared to the overall industrial picture. The age span continued the same, the major concentration being between twenty-one and thirty-three. No one under seventeen worked in the local mines, and only four miners dug past the hoary age of sixty; this continued to be a young man's occupation.

The reason for its remaining a young man's work is not difficult to understand. The stamina and physical labor required had not diminished noticeably since the 1880s. Although the miners pushed for an eight-hour day, it would not become common until the time of World War I. Ten to twelve hours were the norm, although in January 1899, in order to increase production, the underground workers went to a thirteen-hour shift and above-ground laborers to a fourteen. The underground shift was typically shorter; however, one walked to and from the work area on his own time, so it all evened out in the end. Nothing about the dirty, dangerous work changed. Usually working in pairs, coal miners dug, picked, and shoveled in dusty, near-total darkness, which their flickering lights barely penetrated. They followed the vein, sometimes standing, sometimes kneeling or prone, put always enveloped by a cloud of suffocating dust, which had the grim potential of eventually choking off their lives if they stayed with mining. Only the tonnage sent to the surface determined the day's wages; dead work, removing of impurities, and rock and timbering were still done on one's own time, a source of deep frustration. Unless careful inspections were made, this policy often led to cutting safety corners in the scramble to make a decent wage.

As a result, the miner's pay pivoted on two factors: the honesty of the checkweighman, who weighed and credited each car that came to the surface, and whether the company used the 2,000 pound (short) or 2,200 pound (long) ton. Over a long day in the mine, the difference would be noticeable. More than one miner was sure the checkweighman assisted the company by short-pounding the cars.

Something else that could make or break a miner's paycheck was the spot he dug in the mine. As in all mining, there were rich and poor diggings, good coal and "boney slate." The location, either near or far from the surface or main passageway, made a difference, as did the availability of cars. As one old-time coal miner pointed out, if the boss was a good friend, you got a good place and a good turn of cars. If he didn't like you, you might sit there all day and not get a car.

Although there is no evidence that such things happened in Crested Butte, it was not unknown for a miner to offer a bribe to secure an easy place to mine, maybe a jug of whiskey or some company scrip, or going so far as to allow the boss to sleep with one's wife. The nicer she was, the better yet the place, according to coal miner Victor Bazenele, who mined over on the eastern slope.

Pay scales varied during these years. The Colorado Bureau of Labor Statistics found in 1895-96 that the CF&I paid its coal miners $.50 to $.60 per ton and day laborers $2.24 to $2.75. By working steadily, with plenty of cars, a miner could earn $3 to $3.50 per day. Following the long strike, common laborers received $3 for an eight-hour day, and skilled laborers $3.50 to $4. The October 8, 1914, *Elk Mountain Pilot* reported that Crested Butte miners earned more than $100.00 per month and anthracite miners over $150.00. These wages, the article went on to claim, were far better than those of any other Colorado coal mining camp.

Even with improved practices, the company still held the edge as long as miners were paid in scrip. Scrip probably caused as much unrest as any other issue except union recognition. In the form of credit slips and tickets issued in lieu of cash, it was exchangeable at face value in the company store, which had graced Elk Avenue since 1895. Trying to trade scrip elsewhere could be frustrating, since the company might not accept it back at full value, forcing independent merchants to discount it. Thus the miner and his family were compelled to buy at the company store, at company prices, whatever the markup might be. The company store could return a tidy profit to the same people who owned the mine — a convenient arrangement. Miners and their unions protested vehemently against the practice and demanded payment in cash rather than the hated scrip.

The CF&I harvested a good deal of bad press over the scrip question, and in 1899 a state antiscrip law tried to curb the evil. It failed, and the company continued to dodge the issue. Not until the disclosures of the 1914 investigations did scrip finally disappear. CF&I's power was no more nakedly displayed than in the long-running battle over this company "funny money."

A composite picture of the dreary work day and problems that beset the life of the coal miner cannot really do justice to the individual miner. To keep the railroads running, the steel mills smoking, and American homes warm, the Crested Butte miner daily risked his life in a job that was seasonal, even in the best of years. Heartbreak was only an accident away; watching a fellow miner be injured or killed happened too frequently. Even though no major disasters hit Crested Butte after Jokerville, friends and relatives died in mining accidents elsewhere. Mrs. James Stewart lost three sons in the terrible Schofield, Utah mine disaster in 1900. As they did on other occasions, Crested Butte residents held a public meeting, sent a resolution of sympathy, and raised money to be sent to help the bereaved families. The *Pilot*, May 3, reminded its readers of their own 1884 pains, "therefore this town can well realize the awfulness of the Schofield horror." It did not have to be a major calamity to cause grief; Matt Slovunovich lost two brothers in a 1910 explosion at Primero, Colorado. It was all part of the job they called coal mining.

The workers at the smoky, sooty coke ovens were usually overlooked in discussions of mining at Crested Butte. This was an unfair oversight, because the Crested Butte ovens generally ranked fourth or fifth as Colorado coke producers. That they badly trailed the southern fields in total production does not negate the fact that the local coal proved to be much better as a coking fuel. Transportation expenses limited the market, but not the quality of the product.

The census taker of 1900 found nineteen coke oven workers, eleven Italians and eight Austrians. Only six were married. Like their mining co-workers, they ranged in age mostly from the twenties into the thirties. When the mine shut down, they stopped work; when it resumed, they went back. There was no independence inherent in their occupation.

Americans willingly gave up the coke oven jobs to these eastern European immigrants, but not so easily did they relinquish positions in the Big Mine. The competition for jobs led to racial antagonism and some violence, neither unusual in the American coal fields. The arrival in Crested Butte of Slavic immigrants to replace older workers duplicated the general pattern of coal mining in the 1890s. The Slav miner (for Crested Butte, translate this as Austrian and Italian) was enticed by the picture of America as the land of opportunity. He was willing to work for less under less favorable conditions, or so claimed the senior miners, whose bigotry charged the immigrants with lower intelligence, racial inferiority, and general un-American characteristics. The truth is that whatever wages and conditions these immigrants found in America were infinitely better than what they had left behind at home.

From the company's viewpoint, the immigrant's willingness to work poorer seams and maintain himself on less money proved to be a decided blessing. That he brought in a different culture, language, and religious background made no material difference. Heartily disagreeing were the all-American patriots, who railed against this threat to "their America."

At Crested Butte racial tensions surfaced early in the nineties; for example, when Austrian miner John Sodja attacked driver Jimmy Gardner. Although no reasons were given, they were not hard to imagine: a racial slur, repeated harassment, or the preferential treatment of non-Slavic miners by the driver in delivering cars. Though badly hurt, Gardner survived to live a long life in the community. The marshal hurried Sodja off to Gunnison to prevent further trouble. The company which welcomed the new workers also made them convenient scapegoats when trouble arose and fired them at the hint of unionism. Thirty-seven Austrians were dismissed in April 1899 under the pretext of "rooms being over crowded."

The newcomers developed into steady, hard-working, skillful miners, disproving the bigoted comments about them. By 1914, the Big Mine crew was completely dominated by the Slavs, a tremendous stride for them in far less than one generation. Management and supervisory positions still lay beyond their grasp, but advancement was near at hand in those areas, too. These men also provided a firm backbone for the United Mine Workers, something the CF&I had not counted on. They had nowhere to turn for redress of grievances but to the union movement. Many of the traditional American organizations and political safety valves remained unknown to them, or were not open to these foreigners. Once the union acquired organizers who could speak their language, the UMW took wing. To counteract this movement, mining companies went to great lengths to assure a generous racial mixture on every crew, thus preventing close cultural and language ties from developing. In this way, too, they thwarted the union. Crested Butte's mining population in 1900, even made up as it was of Austrians, Italians, English, Irish, Russians, Germans, Belgians, and Americans, was not as cosmopolitan as most coal mining communities.

Not only did these eastern European people come to dominate the Big Mine and nearby smaller ones, but they also changed and colored the life of Crested Butte. Colorado recognized these changes when it printed mining laws in a variety of languages. By 1914 the complexion of Colorado coal mining had been altered because of the quarter-century-old influx of these people, who were called the "new immigrants." Life at the Big Mine went on as usual, work now conducted in a babble of languages that slowly evolved into heavily accented, broken English.

Not all the coal mining in the Crested Butte area was controlled by CF&I. Small operations such as the Horace, Bulkley, and Porter mines had a season or two, maybe more, in the sun, particularly when the CF&I ran into some labor troubles and shut down. They did especially well in 1913-14 but were never able to approximate the Big Mine's production.

These mines' hardships were nothing compared to the trouble that befell the hard-rock mines. How far they had fallen since those exciting, flush days of the early eighties, when they promised the future upon which the Elk Mountain district would flourish. That future had come and gone; their day fled past and flickered away. Though gone, it was not forgotten; unquestionably, the big discovery would soon be made. Hope kept the boys prospecting and digging.

The *Pilot* did its best over the years to pump life into that languishing industry, giving it far more space than it deserved. Optimistic forecasts can be found in almost any year: the mining outlook was the best it had been in five, ten, twenty years; metal prices were bound to be on the rise; the revival was just around the corner; a local mine looked very promising; and so it went. The idea was to promote and boom, never criticize. The editor of the *Pilot* sharply took to task the "knockers," in his May 27, 1902, issue. Knocking a property or company would discourage operations, he warned, close mines, and hurt the industry. It must be ever onward, and damn those who dragged their heels. Indisputably, conditions would improve.

That improvement did not come to pass. The slump evident in the 1880s accelerated in the 1890s, particularly with the international collapse of the price of silver and the long economic depression. Mines that were marginal in the best of times failed during those years. What Crested Butte needed was a smelter, a familiar cry. As late as 1908, this panacea for all mining ills was being widely discussed. With a smelter the low grade silver lead ores could be worked, mining would revive, and a "great epoch of prosperity" would be at hand. Even more far-fetched straws than this were occasionally grasped. One of those times was in 1902, when the *Pilot* seriously proposed establishing a hard-rock miners' union to improve the wages of the laborers and turn the district into a happy place where investors would come and mining would thrive.

Crested Butte's moment on the silver mining stage was gone; no magic elixir could revive it. The town would have to subsist on coal mining as its major industry and economic pillar. This must have been a bitter pill for many to swallow; some prospectors continued to wander among the hills searching for the elusive mother lode. They were eventually forced to accept the fact that coal was and would be king.

Coal left its mark. Crested Butte was not a hard-rock mining community anymore, CF&I saw to that. Coal and coke left another mark, in the form of polluted air that hung over the town. When coal is transformed into coke, sooty smoke pollution results, especially when burned in an open pit, the initial process used in Crested Butte. That smoke and those flames were seen then, not as irritants, but as signs of progress: "at night the place reminded us of a Pittsburgh by being illuminated with the flames from the coke ovens," crowed the *Elk Mountain Pilot*, December 29, 1881 (then safely ensconced at Irwin). Writer Ernest Ingersoll "saw the elephant" a bit later and reacted similarly: "at night, when the blaze of the coke ovens sheds a lurid glare upon the over-hanging woodlands and the snug town, one can appreciate the far-seeing expectations that lead the people there to call their town the Pittsburgh of the West."

"Pittsburgh of the West" was not a bad sounding title for youthful Crested Butte; the town reveled in it. The editor of rival Gothic's *Silver Miner* more cryptically described it as "Smokeyville." Although Crested Butte never became a second

Pittsburgh, the pollution continued. Railroad engineer Lewis Lathrop recalled the sickeningly sweet odor of coal being baked into coke that hung over the town when he worked there in the mid-nineties. Visiting the mines and town in September 1902, mining engineer Thomas A. Rickard commented that the surrounding mountains "gain height and mystery as seen through the smoke from the coke ovens of Crested Butte." Rickard did not like coal mining camps and later dismissed those he had seen in Gunnison County as illustrating "all the hideousness which belongs to those unhappy-looking settlements," Pollution came to be accepted as part of life, not something to complain or worry about unnecessarily. If the sight or smell of it suddenly disappeared, there was immediate concern over why the Big Mine and its ovens had shut down.

Coal mining was not alone in despoiling the land and the air: hard-rock mining contributed its share. Mines and dumps polluted streams, and miners scarred mountainside and valley floor in the relentless search for hidden metals. By 1900 the Elk Mountains clearly showed the effects of twenty years of hard prospecting and mining.

Not everyone approved of such destructive activity. Helen Hunt Jackson was one of the objectors. While watching mining operations approach a beautiful field of purple asters some two miles west of Crested Butte, she mused, as mentioned earlier, that some people would rather have the flowers than the coal on the opposite bank.

> *There is no accounting for differences in values; no adjusting them either, unluckily. The men who are digging, coking, selling the coal opposite the aster field, do not see the asters; the prospectors hammering away high up above the foaming, splashing, sparkling torrent of the O-Be-Joyful water do not know where it is amber and where it is white, or care for it unless they need a drink.*

Jackson cared, but at the moment she defied the rush of time, almost a prophet without followers. She could enjoy the beauty while it lasted; too many others sought only money and metals.

By the turn of the century a growing awareness of the environment was slowly emerging. When the game warden of the district could warn mining companies to stop polluting local streams with tailings and sediments because they destroyed fishing, then times were changing. Local complaints had spurred him into taking action. Not only were polluted streams not good for fishing, but they also were not conducive to tourism, which had the potential for bringing in as much or more money than hard-rock mining.

As attitudes toward the environment changed, so did the world around mountain-sheltered Crested Butte and the Big Mine. The outside world could not be kept out anymore than winter could. As tension mounted in Europe, the *Pilot* conscientiously followed events. Then war came and an era ended. The first reaction was one of anticipation — surely the war would increase demand for high-grade steam coal. Local mines produced the best, and CF&I would be "obliged" to put the Big Mine in operation. Anything that seemed likely to bring the district out of the strike doldrums of 1914 appeared to be a blessing and, if it improved the coal demand, all the better. Little did people know what lay ahead.

CHAPTER 4

Crested Butte is My Home

1892-1914

Years of change, of transition now came to Crested Butte. Its physical appearance changed only slightly, the population rising from around 850 to 988 in 1900, then declining somewhat before rising again in the 1910s. The transformation was evident in the makeup of the population. Several trends emerged; pioneer leadership gave way to a new generation. Many of the old-timers, with enough of those famous winters under their belts to last a lifetime, moved to California. A few returned to the homeland, such as Mr. and Mrs. Jacob Phillips, who went back to South Wales in 1901. More noticeable was the arrival of the new immigrant, discussed in relation to coal mining in the previous chapter.

The eastern European immigrant arrived in Crested Butte in a pattern similar to that of the entire United States, particularly the coal regions. They came tentatively in the late eighties, slowly in the nineties, and full tide by the turn of the century. "First comes man, then a long time nothing, than comes the woman," went an old Slovak saying, which aptly applied to Crested Butte. Margaret Mihelich's experiences explain why. Her fiancé, John Bear, immigrated to America and sent back fare money to the not quite eighteen-year-old Margaret. In April 1899, she left home: "I come myself to Crested Butte. Nobody come with me." After nine seasick days on the ship and five days by train, she arrived: "It was a long trip from Yugoslavia." Regardless of timing, they all came because of the opportunities offered by the town and the mines. As they expressed it, "One came to Colorado and thought it was heaven here compared to the old country."

It took them ten years or more to create an impact. They faced ethnic discrimination here, as elsewhere, though more subtle than open. In the 1890s and early 1900s, their names were printed in the paper more for disturbances of the peace than for commendable actions. For instance, Joseph Celovsky, "ringleader of a gang of Croat-Austrians," was fined $20 for disturbances in March 1900, and Antone Chiedo, two months later, paid $5 and costs for assault and offensive language. To counter balance these negative impressions, leaders who appealed to both old and new Crested Butte were emerging. One of them was twenty-one-year-old Italian Saverio Vecchio. A naturalized citizen, educated in the local schools, he was hailed by the *Pilot* on September 4, 1900, as "a progressive and wide-awake young business man [saloonkeeper] possessing large property interests inherited and earned. His ability and intelligence have made him the leader of the Italian colony in Crested Butte." Two years later, he returned to Italy and brought his family back to America.

These immigrants migrated easily since many, like Vecchio, had no families with them. The post office, among its unclaimed letters, listed such names as Correi, Matkovich, Pollis, and Albo. For these men, a job in one coal mine was as good as another. Their mobility produced much localized intramigration among the various Colorado Slavic communities, thereby cementing broader ties for a group looking for fellowship and trying to put down roots in a new, and in many ways alien, culture.

Colorado Fuel and Iron, which had encouraged so many of them to come to Colorado, recognized its responsibility and attempted to bridge the language and cultural gap. Its publication, *Camp and Plant*, 1901-04, printed short articles in German, Spanish, and Italian, as well as English. The company sought to stimulate a desire for citizenship by providing classes in English, American history, and government in its camps. Its plan succeeded — in April 1903, fifty-two Italians traveled to Gunnison to take out their final naturalization papers, an event the *Pilot* proudly reported. As the years went by, eastern European names appeared ever more frequently in local and society news, business advertisements, politics, and sports. The Crested Butte baseball nine, which routed Marble's team 21-8 in August 1914, was led by such stalwarts as Pasic, Skoff, Byouk, and three Yoklaviches. Once they began their journey, the new immigrants traveled swiftly down the American road to Crested Butte.

The women came along with them. The *Elk Mountain Pilot* (October 29, 1914) notified the wives that once their husbands became citizens, they, too, became so classified and were eligible to vote. Some discussion had apparently arisen over that point with regard to the upcoming election, and the editor wanted it known that wives of all citizens of Crested Butte who had been naturalized had a "perfect right to vote." Anna Kochevar demonstrated their new-found place in the community. Hailed as one of the pioneering Slovakian women, arriving in the late eighties, she was lauded for having raised a fine family of eight children while enduring many hardships. Anna came from Simich, Yugoslavia to Iowa, then to Crested Butte, where she married Joseph Kochevar and established a prominent local family.

The new immigrants' impact on their adopted community proved to be broad and deep. They came and literally conquered. Crested Butte would never be the same again and, despite fears of superpatriots, was neither corrupted nor doomed by their appearance; it gained in vitality and flavor.

The census of 1900 clearly illustrates their growing influence. Austrians (the census taker made no effort to discern differences among the various nationalities that composed the Austrian-Hungarian empire) led the foreign-born contingent by a wide margin, representing 25 percent of the total population. Italians with 8 percent, were second, followed by the English, Scots, Germans, and Irish, these groups together constituting nearly half of the population. They lived in roughly defined ethnic neighborhoods, a typical phenomenon that afforded eastern Europeans a measure of stability and direction in the strange American world. These, combined with the companionship found in ethnic saloons, lodges, and the Catholic church, ameliorated the cultural shock.

Foreigners had already largely replaced Americans as day laborers, coal miners, coke workers, and railroad crews — jobs that demanded physical stamina and a willingness to work under adverse conditions. They were also making inroads into mining engineering, quartz mining, freighting, and main street business. Of fourteen men listed as bartenders or saloonkeepers in 1900, eight came from Italy or Austria, and Austrians, Hungarians, and Italians listed their occupations as merchants; one was even a jeweler. They had not cracked the ranks of professional and white-collar positions — physician, banker, teacher, and minister — and were rarely seen as carpenters, clerks, and cooks.

Refuting charges that they were transients and thus a burden on the community, foreign-born homeowners far outnumbered their American counterparts, indicating a willingness to settle permanently in Crested Butte. The size of turn-of-the-century families amazes Americans today. Thirteen families had ten or more children, and five, six, or seven were not at all uncommon. Not uncommon, either, were a larger number of childhood deaths. It should not be blithely assumed that the Catholic eastern European immigrants exclusively produced the huge families. The thirteen largest families were American or northern European.

Where these immigrants did come from somewhat justified the fears of the overly concerned Americans, who felt foreigners threatened the country's very soul. In the area of literacy, Austrians and Italians led the list of those who could not read, write, or speak English. Nearly 50 percent of the coke workers fell into the illiterate category, reinforcing the point that this occupation served as the first step for the totally unskilled. Both Gunnison County and Crested Butte hovered near the Colorado illiteracy average in 1900, indicating that what occurred here was not unusual. Crested Butte was distinctive in that it attracted many more Austrians than was typical for the state.

In what sounds like the familiar refrain of being undercounted, the *Elk Mountain Pilot*, on July 3, 1900, accused the census enumerators of being neither as thorough nor as accurate as they should have been. Although they found a record high 988 residents, the editor claimed a large number of residents "had not been counted." The only support for this contention was the figure of a thousand or better, which had been tossed around in the nineties and claimed by the Colorado Fuel and Iron after 1900. Which one was right will never be known.

If the makeup of the population changed, the composition of those running the community did not; Colorado Fuel and Iron and the merchants still held the reins. Between them they guided Crested Butte's destiny with steady conservative hands.

Reflecting growth and long-term stability, the business district expanded in the 1890s; in 1897 the list included barbers, real estate and insurance agents, dressmakers, bankers, and general merchants. There were several hotels, saloons, livery stables, blacksmiths, a jeweler, a hardware store, and a confectionery. The owners' names indicated their origins: McCosker, Decker, Chappell, Block, Axtell, Anderson, Metzler, Welch, and so on — only in saloons were eastern European names likely to surface. Fourteen years later, the business district had expanded to include a grocer, photographer, shoemaker, bottling works, restaurant, telephone company, opera house, skating rink, and drug store. The names Chiodo, Kochevar, Kuretich, Niccoli, Oreschnick, and Verzuh indicated that the eastern Europeans had steadily invaded the business community within a very short time. The variety of enterprises conclusively proves that Crested Butte was never a true company town, in spite of its company store, the Colorado Supply.

The "old guard" was giving way now; only V.F. Axtell was still active. George Holt had long ago returned to Illinois, and Howard Smith, who really started it all but had never achieved the success he hoped for, was reported in 1902 to be living in Elkhart, Indiana. Others, such as pioneering newspaperman John Phillips, merchants Marcellus J. Gray and Sam Brust, and one of the first public school teachers, Mrs. Bessie Webster, retired to southern California, where a colony of former Crested Butte folks had formed. Some, like one-time town marshal, mayor, and merchant John Tetard, had died.

In their places emerged the Glick brothers and Victor Metzler, transitional figures, who came in the 1880s and were still active in the 1900s. Jerry Olney got his start in Crested Butte as manager of the Colorado Supply Company store and liked the town so well that he resigned from CF&I and stayed to operate a clothing store until his death in 1903. That genial New Yorker, Daniel Miner, who had faced the onslaught of Pickett's charge at Gettysburg on a hot July day in '63 and later marched through Georgia with Sherman, ran a livery stable until 1906, when he decided to turn to ranching in Adams County. This lifelong Republican served one term as county commissioner and twenty-five years as a local businessman. In 1900, thirty-five-year-old Scotsman and ex-trustee John Arnott became city marshal, a job now less pressure-filled than it was earlier, drunks and dogs being the principal culprits.

Dr. John W. Rockefeller proved to be one of the most enterprising of Crested Butte's leaders. From the medical profession he branched out into ownership of the light and water company and in 1911 became one of the owners of the bank. An energetic and businesswise man of the "strictest integrity," he maintained the bank's high standard of stability and service. Young Dr. Orlando Oram came to absorb some of the medical practice that Rockefeller relinquished when his interests broadened.

A most interesting person to appear in this bastion of male leadership was lanky Sylvia Smith, a strong-willed crusading newspaper editor, who published the *Weekly Citizen* from 1900-07. "Success to you, Sister Smith," greeted the rival *Pilot* in August, a questionably sincere wish. Charles Ross, leaving as editor and publisher of the *Pilot*, showed the depth of feeling in April 1902 by leveling this blast at "Soapy old Gal," a not-too-subtle reference to the notorious con man Soapy Smith: "we cannot but overlook the harmless ranting of our passé maiden sister of the frigid heart. One whose nature is so permeated with the man's pants because she could not get a pair already filled." Ignoring these prejudices, she served a term as town clerk and recorder in 1906, and her newspaper was selected several times to do the city's printing. Sylvia agitated the community repeatedly by taking on the D&RG, the Colorado Supply, and CF&I, for reasons now lost, as are the issues of her paper. She eventually left, moving to Marble, and ran into a hornet's nest of trouble for her unflagging zeal and caustic editorials. The *Pilot* went about its business of promoting, defining, giving advice, editorializing, and occasionally making some reform outbursts of its own. It always looked to the future with confidence.

Smith stood out as one of the few women in Crested Butte's masculine business and professional world. Even with attitudes toward women liberalizing, they found themselves limited to traditional businesses and occupations: notions and millinery stores, dressmaking, management of a boarding house, restaurant, or hotel (which, translated, most likely meant cook), "servants," waitresses, and chambermaids. One would occasionally break out of the mold, as did Mrs. M.J. Boyle, who managed the bottling works with its soda water and soft drinks. Teaching was their only professional outlet. Economically, their impact was felt mostly in the roles of housewife and mother, certainly critical factors in the success of the community. More women lived in Crested Butte in 1914 than twenty years before, but their impact proved no greater. This indicates not only the general attitude of the day, but also the role of women in eastern European culture and its transmission to Crested Butte with the immigrants. It would take a while to change established patterns.

As they had in the past, merchants dominated city government, either by running for office or working behind the scenes to insure the victory of candidates who held similar views. City elections came and went routinely, unless a candidate or issue challenged accepted ideas or practices. The 1899 election drew attention when the usually dominant Republicans fell to fighting, and three parties entered tickets in the race. Caucuses, rallies, and speeches occupied March and early April. The issues varied from the battling women of the WCTU who desired to defeat a saloon man to the *Pilot's* cry for economical government. Charges that boys under fifteen were voting in the caucuses and stuffing ballot boxes enlivened the proceedings. Interest mounted and perfect election day weather turned the voters out in record numbers. They proved to be independently inclined, selecting winning candidates from all tickets and basing their decisions on how well known or qualified a candidate was rather than on the issues involved. Crested Butte then returned to normal.

Several years later, in 1908, passions were aroused during a campaign by the "law abiding peace and morality loving people" against the saloon crowd over the controversial issues of Sunday closing, saloon licenses, and women frequenting and working in saloons. The *Pilot* breathed a sigh of relief when most of the voters agreed to protect Crested Butte's morality and community image. Finally, in 1914, following charges and countercharges of election day disturbances, the winning candidates sponsored a free dance for the public. This seemed to defuse ill-humored accusations, amid the whirl of dancers and an evening of sociability.

State and national elections sometimes proved to be equally lively but with serious overtones. Crested Butte voters left no doubt where they stood in 1902 on the Eight-Hour-Day

Amendment — 199 for, 17 against. The women of the United Congregational Church took advantage of Election Day 1908 to raise money by serving meals. The voters ate well, and the ladies realized "in the neighborhood of $70." The *Elk Mountain Pilot*, a determined Republican paper, played a significant political role, even when annoyed with its own party's president, Theodore Roosevelt. His withdrawal of public land deprived the miner and homesteader of opportunities for success, a policy that did not endear T. R. to the paper or to many local people. Showing its feisty spirit, the *Pilot* also blasted the 1911 Colorado legislature for "doing nothing but bickering with making and unmaking propositions while nobody could depend on any thing, as what was done one day was torn up and thrown in the waste basket the next day." The paper also took on the county commissioners over the long standing problem of county roads.

Crested Butte people with political ambitions apart from the town found themselves working from a weak base. They did pick up a few county offices, such as that won by dedicated Pat Hanlon, hailed as the "most popular" marshal the town ever had. He was elected Gunnison County sheriff in 1908 and moved to Gunnison with the good wishes of the community he left behind.

In Crested Butte, city government fell into a familiar pattern. Year after year the board of trustees approved appropriations of $6,000 for three funds: water and light, fire and police, and general. That took care of expenses. Routine matters filled the minutes of the meetings: liquor licenses, the use of the council room for meetings, dog licenses, and the annual squabble over the spring cleanup of homes and alleys. Mysteriously terse comments occasionally piqued interest: "The board then remained two hours longer and debated on the questions of grasshoppers, crickets, whistles and the big fire." The trustees donated money for the July 4 celebration, listened to citizens' complaints, anguished over health conditions, and wrestled with the continuing problem of safe sidewalks, finally resolving in 1910 that cement sidewalks were the answer. Crested Butte's problems were those of its contemporaries.

Amid all the cheers for the successes of American democracy, more than a few Crested Butte citizens became concerned about socialism, an obviously un-American product of foreign infiltration. In his October 28, 1902, story on the appearance of the socialist candidate for Lieutenant Governor, the reporter for the *Pilot* was forced to admit that some good ideas came forth, but he qualified his admission by stating that the speech was more interesting than practical, and that many of the ideas were not at all fitted to present needs and conditions. He also took pains to call attention to the small audience for the speech in City Hall. Although socialism seemed far removed from mountain protected Crested Butte, neither the mountains nor anything else could keep it from taking root there. Within a year, socialists were holding regular meetings and candidates, and eventually whole slates began to appear in local elections.

Seldom did the socialists enjoy the same success as in 1914, when they nominated Dr. Orlando Oram for mayor; Paul Panian, Jacob Kochevar, and B.F. Bennett for trustees; John McIntyre, clerk; John Starika, treasurer; and John Nemenic, town marshal. Characterizing themselves as the party of the people and campaigning on a regular socialist platform, including public ownership of "all those things upon which people in common depend," they swept the election. This unprecedented ethnic ticket surprised the *Pilot* and many others but did not reflect a wholesale turn to socialism. The labor troubles of 1913-14 swelled the party's ranks as did general dissatisfaction with the way the American dream was turning out.

The Colorado Fuel & Iron hoped to avoid political skirmishing, because its goal for the American dream — profit — seemed right on track. Nineteen-fourteen, however, was not a good year for the company, and it had more things to occupy its corporate mind than a local election in Crested Butte. In general, though, it watched over the community with a careful eye and involved itself in a number of different ways.

One of those ways was local politics, but the degree of its involvement cannot be determined. Even the *Pilot*, seldom overly critical of CF&I, commented on March 24, 1910, that Crested Butte had two classes of Republicans: "one is called the 'C.F.&I.' while the other is 'Independents'; the former vote for 'corporation' and the latter vote 'as they please.'" The company preferred to work behind the scenes, out of the glare of the political spotlight. Whether the company encouraged its people to become locally involved is also not known, but at least one did. Scotsman Andrew Alexander, Big Mine superintendent, who worked up from fire boss at the time of the 1891 strike, served several terms as trustee and one as mayor, 1901-03. Apparently kindly and well-liked, he represented the best that the company sent to the mine and town. When CF&I transferred him in the fall of 1905, the trustees approved this motion in tribute to "his good and faithful service":

> *Whereas it is the desire of this board upon behalf of the people in general, to testify to his long and valuable service as a public officer, his sterling integrity as a citizen, and strong character as a father & husband; therefore, be it resolved that the board of trustees of the town of Crested Butte have [tendered] a vote of thanks to Mr. Andrew Alexander as a token of regards and appreciation for his services, public & private, to this town and its people.*

"On the coal mining industry has hinged the wealth or woe of the camp," observed the *Pilot* as 1901 drew to a close. With nearly 400 employed at the Big Mine and a payroll approaching half a million dollars, the paper could not have more nearly hit the truth. All of this impact, of course, translated into Colorado Fuel and Iron, whose chief symbol, besides the mine, was its business counterpart, the Colorado Supply Company on Elk Avenue.

The original supply company had been started by CF&I founder John Osgood and others in 1888, the same year its first store was opened at Sopris, Colorado. With the merger and creation of CF&I, operations expanded to all coal communities. For Crested Butte, this meant 1895, before the company store arrived. Controversy over the "pluck me stores" has aroused impassioned debate. "There is a damnable outrage worked by many coal mining companies upon their poor, ignorant and almost helpless miners," stormed the *Mining Industry* in 1894. The Colorado Supply made a specialty of catering to miners' trade, coolly answered CF&I; the store and use of scrip benefit the miner and his family as much as they the employer. The two went together, the store and the scrip, and although it denied that either was compulsory, CF&I pressured workers into patronizing one and accepting the other. Without question, Colorado Supply had a monopoly in many CF&I camps, though not in Crested Butte, and returned a profit for the parent company.

In Crested Butte, the Colorado Supply Company store advertised itself as Gunnison County's largest, which it well may have been at the turn of the century. Its stock, ranging from shoes to furniture to groceries, was the widest available, and its manager Jerry Olney claimed "reasonable prices" as the secret to its success. The manager, the most important individual, owned stock in the company, and Olney was one of the most popular and successful managers at Crested Butte. Although set back by being burned out in May 1901, the company quickly leased a building, brought in new merchandise, and laid plans for future construction. It soon regained its position within the business community and remained the major store for the rest of Crested Butte's coal mining era. It advertised in December 1910:

Get in Touch with a LIVE HOUSE
in your Hometown to do Your Trading.
Try US for a Live One, and Be CONVINCED.

Our Competitors May Dilly Dally in Our Smoke
But Can Not Get On Our Firing Line.

Quality, Quantity and Prices Unequaled by Any Concern.
Each and Every Article GUARANTEED.
If Not Satisfactory, Money Refunded.

Aside from merchandising, the Colorado Supply wielded substantial influence in the coal camps. Should the store manager ally himself with the mine superintendent, the two of them could control much of the political, economic, and social life. This alliance, along with high prices and monopoly, created repeated anti-company agitation, particularly in 1913-14. Interestingly, these factors did not play a large role at Crested Butte. Competition and the failure of CF&I to dominate mitigated the company's local impact and curbed the ruthlessness. The independent heritage of the hard-rock era never yielded completely to CF&I.

Besides the obvious store and mine, CF&I actively involved itself in Crested Butte's life in other ways. The company hired a local physician to handle minor medical matters while maintaining its hospital at Pueblo for more serious cases. At Christmas, chocolates and/or other confections were distributed to the children, who thought of the CF&I as a benevolent Santa Claus. Another charitable gesture involved a $100 donation to the Union Congregational Church for fencing and painting the parsonage. The company also built and rented housing, although it never monopolized the real estate market.

Much of this philanthropy was administered by the company's sociological department, which also published the company magazine, *Camp and Plant*. Among the department's goals were improvement of housing, sanitary conditions, and education, provision for social gatherings; and establishment of adult classes — all commendable. Among other things it did were employ kindergarten teachers, organize a circulating library, exhibit art collections, and publish articles on such varied topics as hygiene, milk and its care, and preparation of foods. Though its achievements often fell short of its goals and CF&I was routinely denounced for its company towns, particularly in southern Colorado, Crested Butte seems to have been one of its shining examples. Given a better social foundation upon which to build in Crested Butte (the southern Colorado coal communities, for example), CF&I did much to improve the quality of life for the residents.

All these actions did not reflect pure altruism. The company strove to enhance its own public image. Issues of *Camp and Plant* paint an almost idyllic picture of the coal communities, none more so than Crested Butte, an unusually "pleasant town of 1,100" with electric lights, waterworks, well-equipped fire department, schools, churches, clubs, societies, and forty business enterprises on "firm financial footing." A dissatisfied state of mind caused by lack of recreation and rational amusement, the enraptured writer went on to say, was next to impossibility. This state of satisfaction was directly attributable to coal mining, so stable an industry that people had attained a degree of "progression and permanence that can only come through prosperity and contentment." The Garden of Eden had been rediscovered at Crested Butte, in the opinion of CF&I.

The facts of life at that time somewhat substantiated the claim. Local coal mining was especially healthy around the turn of the century; not until 1908 did it slump badly, rallying again before the bottom dropped out in strike-dominated 1914. The 1893 crash and following depression years hurt mainly because the closing of Colorado's silver mines and smelters cut into the coal market. An awesome shock initially rattled the district. Some 500 persons were thrown out of work, and a mood of despondence prevailed. Only one Crested Butte business failed, however, and most of the unemployed were out-of-work silver miners. Several years passed before prosperity returned, and when it did, it smiled as seldom before. In 1900 the *Pilot* hailed the year just past and looked ahead toward boom, progress, and banner growth. Crested Butte rode out a brief late 1907-08 national banking panic with aplomb, thanks to "conservative management."

Though perhaps never quite living up to its advance 1880 billing, the "coal mining center of western Colorado" had survived, nevertheless. Where now were Gothic, Irwin, Schofield, and the rest of its early rivals?

Thanks to the railroad and the development of local ranching and some farming, the cost of living stayed at moderate levels. While 1900 prices for hamburger, $.08 a pound; potatoes, $.01 each; rice, $.07 a pound; ham, $.18 a pound, eggs; $.20 a dozen; boys' shoes, $.90; bath towels, 4 for $.25; and men's pants at $2 seem like unbelievable bargains now, it should be remembered that wages fluctuated at corresponding levels. Only once, so far as is known, did one of the festering problems of coal mining, irregular paydays, plague Crested Butte. That was in 1895, not the best of times, when almost every citizen in town signed a petition for monthly paydays. The company apparently agreed to the demand, and the issue died.

To continue on down the *Camp and Plant*'s list of community attributes, Crested Butte could be proud of its school. Rock School, built in '83, was crowded with 225 scholars in 1900, taught by three teachers, according to the county superintendent of schools. That would have produced some incredibly large classes, unless, as is likely, 225 was the number of eligible pupils, not those in daily attendance. In 1911 a new eight-room building relieved the overcrowding. By 1914 plans were afoot to provide ten grades at Crested Butte, the nearest high school being in Gunnison, and a manual training department, both steps in the right direction.

The *Pilot* repeatedly extolled the local schools and teachers. At the end of the school year in June 1912, accolades were awarded to teachers for their energy and discipline, to the parents for their cooperation, and to the magnificent new school building, the "gem of the town." Parents could not have wished for a more well-conducted, disciplined school. However, the same paper was forced to admit in October 1913 that unruly students contributed to the principal's nervous breakdown. A replacement arrived and promised to take "hold with a firm hand;" the school board pledged just as firmly to uphold him in that plan. Some parents saw no need for their children to receive so much book learning, and, on at least one occasion (January 23, 1900), the *Pilot* pleaded with them not to allow their children to drop out of school.

The Union Congregational and St. Patrick's Catholic churches represented the religious world confronting the secular world of Crested Butte. The Catholic Church steadily acquired members from among the new immigrants until it was nearly ready for a resident priest. The Congregationalists, on the other hand, had a minister only intermittently, reflecting their somewhat precarious position in the community. Perhaps their outstanding clergyman was the Reverend James Kyle "beloved for his sterling qualities as a man." Moving on, he was eventually elected as a United States Senator from South Dakota, a deserved distinction, according to the *Pilot*. The Methodists sought to attract a following at Crested Butte without lasting success. The Gunnison pastor served that constituency on a circuit basis.

Churches, always good for a community's image, had a debatable impact on community life. As the years went by, they offered more congregational and individual help, then branched out into community-wide service, the typical pattern for Colorado mining towns. One of their most effective functions was to help the immigrant find a mooring in his new world; thus, as the complexion of Crested Butte's population changed, the Protestant influence receded. This, of course, upset the old line, one hundred percent Protestants, who were frustrated by their inability to maintain the status quo.

Part of the church's role was assumed by the increased number of fraternal lodges and societies during these years. The familiar ones were there: Odd Fellows, Masons, Knights of Pythias, and Woodmen of the World for the men; Rebekahs and Rathbone Sisters for the women. The eastern Europeans brought their societies with them, and by 1903 they included St. Joseph, Ban Jelacic Lodge, the Croation Sisters of St. Mary, and St. Mary's Lodge. All these organizations fostered a sense of belonging and individual worth in a growingly impersonal world, as well as providing the ever-popular social activities. No easier entry into a new community could be made by an individual than through his or her lodge or society. Working up through the various degrees gave a sense of importance available nowhere else.

Cultural activities offset the CF&I-created industrial image of Crested Butte. City Hall served as the center for those activities. Some of the ongoing "crucial" issues that faced the city fathers were whether to purchase a piano, which they finally did in 1912 after much wrangling, and how much rent to charge per night for the hall. That controversial piano was not the community's only one — the *Pilot* proudly mentioned the town's eighteen organs and nineteen pianos in 1900.

That same year, during the height of the cultural season (the winter months), the newspaper reported an active dancing school, parlor concerts by the Union Congregational choir, performances of the local dramatic club that drew large crowds to City Hall, and dramas by a traveling troupe, which played to a full house. Large cities might scoff at these kinds of cultural offerings, but Crested Butte was delighted with them. The *Pilot*, on February 20, 1900, pondered the fact that "Crested Butte is a good show town and it is a strange thing that more attractions don't make this point." Not many "made the point," because the potential audience was never large enough. Should an inferior company land in town, however, both the paper and the audience let it know their feelings.

Crested Butte folks created most of their own cultural life. Occasionally, a town band enlivened the evenings with practice and performances. Starting in 1901, "phonograph concerts" were a popular form of entertainment. The Colorado Supply store, in 1910, advertised the arrival of 200 "disc talking machine records to fit any disc machine." Motion pictures were introduced with an exhibition in 1902, and in 1912 the Isis Theater conducted a drawing to lure more patrons to its shows. Subsequent cultural offerings were typical for a mountain-locked Colorado mining community, but certainly better than those of the neighboring foothill coal mining camps, which lacked Crested Butte's strong middle class independent character.

The community had better-than-average water and electrical service, although not as good as the CF&I writer implied. Not until 1899 did the *Pilot* compliment the light and water company for not closing down for even one night during the winter, "a condition unprecedented in the history of the town." The council was forever asking why the company failed to furnish power according to its contract. It was easy to blame the company, but it encountered problems of its own: abominable winters, poor equipment, and a market too small to stand the cost of expansion and modernization. In 1908, Dr. Rockefeller and others purchased the company and soon installed a new dynamo, nearly doubling current capacity. Under new ownership, conditions improved, and the little hydroelectric plant better served community needs.

Part of the company's responsibility was to supply water, a particularly difficult problem in the face of the typical freezing winters. Improved equipment, however, led to three winters of water uninterrupted by frozen mains and pipes. That record was set in the late 1890s, too late to prevent a second devastating fire in the early morning hours of January 9, 1893. The fire companies raced to the blaze, only to find water mains frozen. Again the business heart of town lay in ruins, partly because of the fire and partly because of the over-enthusiastic use of 150 pounds of dynamite. The blast knocked in one side of City Hall and demolished many buildings. Windows shattered throughout town, turning many a warm, snug harbor into an icebox. Unfortunately, many of the buildings were uninsured.

January seemed to be the month for fires. On Saturday morning, January 7, 1899, shouts of fire, pistol shots, and the clanging of the fire bell alerted the town. This time prompt action by the fire laddies and functioning water system limited damage to one destroyed building, the "best fitted" saloon in town. Though its patrons grieved, the loss proved much less traumatic to the general population.

A third major fire hit the business district in May 1901, resulting in the Colorado Supply store and several other buildings going up in flames. This time the fire company was handicapped by not enough hose but was aided by better weather conditions and a wind-free morning.

Crested Butte's dismal record of fires was not unusual, nor was the fact that many of them occurred in winter when stoves and pipes tended to overheat or malfunction in some other way. Stringent city ordinances attempted to control these dangers. The fire companies did their best and, when all went well, were able to check the fire's spread and limit the damage. When not fighting fires, the firemen were enthusiastic participants in the social whirl of the community, and not so bad in hose races either.

Transportation was limited to the train and horse throughout most of these years. Sufficient most of the time, they were not always perfect. Several times the paper editorially scolded the D&RG for the lack of cars, inconsiderate actions toward passengers, and generally ignoring the community. The railroad did not bother to respond, clearly indicating where Crested Butte stood in its scheme of things. Then a "new boy," the automobile, moved onto the block. By 1911-12, Crested Butte was caught up in an "automobile rage," even to the point of providing bus service to and from the depot. Newspaper stories described adventuresome trips to the county seat. A sure sign of the town's progressiveness, the automobile, it was hoped, meant that good roads were coming too. Cars motored beautifully in late spring, summer, and fall, but when the snow came, it was time to put them up on blocks and hitch up the sleigh.

All these innovations helped make life easier for the average Crested Butte resident as the years rolled by. A larger business district meant more selection for Christmas gifts, from toys to chinaware. This was one time of the year, too, when the churches played a communitywide role with programs, special services, and joyful music. Thanks to local merchants and hard working people, some memorable July Fourth celebrations featured orations, sports events, grand balls, and fireworks. Nothing heartened locals more than to have the town nine defeat rival Gunnison, which they did in 1911, 14-10. Other holidays were less important. Bad weather dampened many an Easter, keeping those bonnets indoors and canceling the "parade." Halloween was for the kids and their pranks, with parties for less rambunctious youngsters. Memorial Day's significance slipped away with the decimated ranks of the "Boys in Blue."

Baseball held onto its place as the number one sport; a defeat was taken as a blow to local pride. The *Elk Mountain Pilot*, July

4, 1912, pulled no punches when the team played Gunnison, a game ending "as usual in our defeat, not through the fault of our players but rather through lack of good management." Five automobiles and a special train brought home a load of dejected fans. For those who preferred other sports, a tennis club was organized in 1910 and a court built. Boxing matches stayed confined to the men's domain, not an appropriate family activity. Physical fitness and athletics were popular by 1911, resulting in the creation of the Crested Butte Athletic Association, which proposed to equip a gym, provide a reading room, and sponsor dances. The *Pilot* tried to shame CF&I into helping underwrite the costs. Other big coal companies did such things, but whether CF&I cooperated is not known. Out of this movement came a community guild hall, built in 1913-14 near the north end of Fourth Street. A multipurpose building, it served for everything from box socials to band concerts, and basketball to indoor baseball. Part of the structure incorporated the old Presbyterian Church from Irwin, hauled down from there to Crested Butte. Enthusiasm for basketball failed to overcome inexperience, and the local team was slaughtered 92-9. Again, it was Gunnison that did them in.

Out in the valley ranching and dairying took hold, providing meat, butter, milk, and cream to enhance local menus and make some locally famous "delicious cream taffy." In its place, a dairy was acceptable, but that place was not in town, as would-be developers found out in 1901. Irate citizens petitioned the trustees to prevent its establishment, and the marshal was instructed to notify the parties to desist from building. Not too far away from Crested Butte could be found farms and orchards, which in season sent into market everything from potatoes to peaches.

Residents were not the only ones who appreciated Crested Butte's natural attributes. Tourists were beginning to arrive in large numbers, attracted by the scenery, the summer climate, and the hunting and fishing. The *Pilot* grasped the significance of that potential industry early, praising local attractions and counting the blessings of increased tourism. Although 1910 plans for an extensive health and pleasure resort never materialized, the Elk Mountain Hotel advertised itself as a "good refreshing summer home for tourists and families at reasonable rates."

Tourism was fine, but even the *Pilot* realized it could adversely affect the local economic base, as in 1910 when an injunction was filed against quartz mills that were polluting streams. This threat to hard-rock mining, with which the paper had carried on a much longer love affair than with tourism, caused the editor to explode on August 18:

> . . . or until such time as we learn to discriminate which is the better for our country, gold as taken from the earth, calling for a large pay roll, or a clear stream on which the fancy fisherman can cast his gaudy fly instead of fishing with the lowly worm.

In the long run, the fly would win out over the worm; the gold to be mined from the tourists' pocketbooks would far surpass that of the mines.

Lest one fall into the promotional trap of thinking Crested Butte was heaven on earth, it should be pointed out that there existed another side of the picture. The CF&I did not describe the soot, dust, and dirt that came along with the coke and coal industries. Nor did the fierce winter weather receive much attention. Thoughtless residents continued to litter, an annoyance the *Pilot* emphasized in its repeated calls for cleanup campaigns. Typical was a July 22, 1909, article on the connection between garbage, flies, and health, which ended with the admonition that Crested Butte could be made a most healthful city with a little painstaking effort by the people and city authorities. At various times, the editor also pushed for lawns and shade trees, two environmentally doomed enterprises.

Although *Camp and Plant* praised the "hygienic" conditions, healthy population, and nearly epidemic-free environment, it was more wishful thinking than a statement of fact. In 1899-1900 an astonishing number of children died, diphtheria being particularly rampant from January to March of 1899. In a day and time when removal of an appendix was a serious operation and fear of scarlet fever closed schools, children were threatened by a multitude of diseases and illnesses. Growing up in Crested Butte could be hazardous to one's health.

Confronted with no major criminal problem, the city fathers, the police, and the ordinary citizen were, nevertheless, nagged by petty crimes. Most of them involved vagrancy, vandalism, drunkenness, youthful pranks (funny and otherwise), "peddler

nuisance," debt evaders, petty thievery, and violation of city ordinances (from dog tax to minors in saloons). These kept the police
busy and sometimes crowded the jail. A goodly portion of these
offenses could be laid at the doorstep of Crested Butte's small
red-light district, which might better be called a saloon district,
stretching along Second Avenue north to Elk Avenue. "Sporting
ladies" did work in Crested Butte, though never in the numbers
of prosperous hard-rock camps. They occasionally made the
paper, which usually chose to downplay their activities In at least
one city election,1908, they were a hot issue. Allusions to sex, a
taboo subject in the Victorian era, became more blatant as attitudes changed. In 1914 the *Pilot* openly advertised Sexual
Knowledge, an illustrated, 320-page book for one dollar, sent in
a plain wrapper. Don't let the neighbors know!

As important as saloons were to the life of the community
and miners, they created their share of problems and raised the
cost of law enforcement. Licensing, patrolling, enforcing Sunday
closing, and like matters needed constant attention. The *Pilot*
expressed the feeling that so many saloons damaged the civic
image. Responding on January 17, 1899, to an article about
Ouray's having one saloon for every 150 people, the paper
remarked:

> *You have nothing to brag about brother. Here in Crested
> Butte we have 13 saloons and a population of 1,000, or one
> saloon for every 77 population. We have only one resident
> minister of the gospel.*

Considering local attitudes, it was surprising that the statewide
prohibition fight, which ended in a 1914 victory for the dries,
produced little local newspaper interest. The *Pilot*, which had
previously taken a stand against prohibition as not the proper
remedy, could say only "aren't you glad it's over?" Perhaps the
aftermath of the great strike and the coming of the war dulled
appreciation for what had just happened.

Crested Butte did not prove to be the gateway to prosperity
for the fledgling merchant, as Martin Kraschovertz found out
when his grocery failed in January 1900. As the newspaper
observed, the grocery business was not all profit and pleasure.
There was tragedy in other areas, too. John Bloznic committed

suicide over his heavy drinking and his wife's leaving him. Michael Cashion, who worked at the coal mine in 1886 or 1887, disappeared, and his sister wrote the paper to look for him twenty-five years later. Then there were the ailments which plagued young and old alike, if the patent medicine ads can be trusted. Aching feet, nervousness, morning tiredness, torpid liver, dandruff, disorders of the feminine organs, gray hair and whiskers, deafness, lumbago, colds, catarrh, coughs, and just old-fashioned aches and pains had their sufferers. If they believed what they read, a cure was only a few cents away.

This was Crested Butte, not quite as CF&I portrayed it, though certainly not so bad as the "typical" Pennsylvania or southern Colorado company town, with its overcrowding, pollution, complete company dominance, unsightliness, and debilitating social, cultural, and political environments. Corporation greed spawned some hideous by-products. Thanks to a fortunate set of circumstances, Crested Butte avoided the worst of these.

Pleasure and pain characterized life for the people who called Crested Butte home. Like stars, these varied elements all converged in 1913-14 with the strike, mine shutdown, people pulling together to weather the crisis, the warm fall weather, the prohibition vote, and the festering European situation. Crested Butte readers, many first-generation immigrants, followed the events, and when the guns roared, in August 1914, they could follow developments with maps, photographs, and front-line reporting. The war was at hand — the war that the *Pilot* hoped would never come now that the "aeroplane" had dropped a bomb that made such a conflict "so hideous" that peace would be promoted. As far away as the fighting was at the moment, its impact on Crested Butte would prove to be much greater than simply an enlarged coal market.

Years of Continuity,
Years of Change
1915-1929

The cheers of glad hearts greeted the Big Mine's whistle in May 1915 when it resounded through the town and echoed down the canyons, proclaiming the reopening of the mine. It had been shut down a long time, eighteen months, and it took more months to reach full operation — not until November could the community rejoice unrestrictedly. The heritage of the camp's longest strike lingered a while longer, but vacant houses slowly refilled and business gradually perked up.

Having lost its claim as the Gunnison Country's premier coal mine in 1906, Crested Butte now stayed locked into the number two position for better than a decade. Somerset, sitting over the mountains to the northwest, had superseded it. The 200,000-ton production years slipped far into the past for the Big Mine. The *Pilot* boldly predicted on February 22, 1917: "War or no War, prosperous times are scheduled for our town of Crested Butte. The coal and metal mines will see an era of activity such as [has] not been known here since the boom days of '79 and '80." That era would not come to pass. Not only that, local history had taken on a rosy glow with the passage of years; it had not been all that good in '79 and '80.

The war did raise production up to the 140,000-ton level. Within four years, however, it was half that, before rallying as the 1920s ended. Shrinking markets and older, more obsolete mining methods and equipment took their toll. The newer Somerset mine, with about 50 percent more men, produced two to three times more tonnage annually, and its location offered easier access to the main line of the Denver and Rio Grande than did still narrow-gauge-locked Crested Butte.

Crested Butte did not worry at first. It basked in a "remarkable revival," a time of "humming" production. Before it could be long enjoyed the twenties set in, with "slack work," a "slow season," and reduced work weeks. The state coal mine inspector was forced to admit in 1929 that markets had shrunk for the whole state, and rigid economy measures had become necessary. Crested Butte did not suffer alone. The optimistic newspaper comments bore an eerie resemblance to those applied to earlier troubles — the ones that tried to buoy hard-rock mining a generation before to keep up the faith and entice investors.

If coal mining could be described as in a decline, coke production had reached a state of collapse. Not until 1917 did Crested Butte show any production, and then only from fifty-two ovens; the last output came in 1918, the end of an era. Thereafter no more sooty, smoky pollution, no glare from the ovens, which once heralded the new "Pittsburgh," despoiled the environment. The closing of the Salida smelter, a prime customer, higher transportation costs, and changes in industrial methods and fuels ended the demand for Crested Butte coke. Its long-ago dual pillar of the economy, hard-rock mining, did not rally and remained as it had for years, only promising better times. One brief 1917 flurry of activity marked a mining departure into the little-understood world of oil shale; nothing came of it. Crested Butte seemed to be starting down the same road taken by Irwin and Gothic decades before. Although some discouraging signs pointed ominously in that direction, that time had not yet come.

Mining went on much as it had before for the men at the Big Mine. Here and elsewhere CF&I miners still labored with picks, even though coal mining throughout the United States had, for the most part, become mechanized. This lack of modernization indicated primarily the mine's gaseous condition and the heavy cost of conversion. In Crested Butte, there might have also been doubt about the ability of the electric company to furnish adequate and continuous power. Finally, in October 1929, work began to electrify the Big Mine to make it the "best equipped, most modern coal mine in the entire state," according to the *Pilot*.

An earlier 1920 study of the entire CF&I coal mining empire found two classes of miners: "piece workers," who were paid by the ton for coal dug and loaded into a car, and "day workers," paid by the day (drivers, motormen, machinists, blacksmiths, tracklayers, and others necessary for coal mining.)Three "bosses" oversaw all the work: the mine foreman, in charge of underground operations; the fire boss, acting as the local safety inspector; and the superintendent, in charge of production and general management of the mine. A simple organization, but it worked well at Crested Butte.

Some things had changed since the great strike. Foremen apparently no longer accepted bribes for the "best rooms;" at least the investigators, Ben Selekman and Mary Van Kleeck, failed to discover any evidence that they did. The investigators did, however, encounter some of the same old complaints about dead work and "equal turn of cars," and also heard charges that foremen were "unfair," something extremely difficult to judge. In the end, they concluded that coal mining was essentially a "dirty, unpleasant, and extremely hazardous occupation." The same words would have described coal mining of a generation before and after. Unable to comprehend why men were attracted to it, they finally decided that its difficulties created the challenge of a "man-sized task."

It wasn't pay that lured men underground at Crested Butte. In 1916 the State Coal Inspector pointed out that the $.58 per ton being paid the miners made it one of the lowest rates in Colorado. CF&I raised wages by ten percent in April 1917, which helped some. By the early twenties some of the higher paid day workers reached the $7.75 per day level. By then both groups were paid by the day with miners nearing five dollars. Apparently miners had a choice, however, of day wages or tonnage.

In 1925, CF&I lowered them twenty percent, a decision for which they would reap trouble in a few years. The company argued that competition from lower paying eastern and New Mexico mines forced the wage reduction.

Frequent complaints of short weeks emerged during these years, meaning that, even with better wages, the yearly totals probably did not increase noticeably. These conditions motivated some miners to move; others simply migrated between the Big Mine and smaller local operations, such as the Bulkley, Horace, and Smith Hill Mines. The one that seemed to offer the best opportunity at the moment drew a few miners from the Big Mine. Although the wages might have been more attractive, the working conditions proved to be more dangerous in these small mines. From 1916 through 1929, only five men were killed in the Big Mine, while the other three, with smaller crews, lost a total of ten. Even one death could be considered too many, but Crested Butte's record was good for Colorado coal mining, especially in light of the fact that in 1917, 188 miners lost their lives, 121 in an explosion at the Hastings Mine in Las Animas County.

For the families of Peter Funaro, John Somrak, and William Grant, statistical evidence provided no consolation. They worked and died for the Colorado Fuel and Iron Company, which — since the 1913-14 strike and its repercussions — had involved itself more with its miners and their work as well as the town itself. When CF&I was found sponsoring a Labor Day celebration, as it did in 1916, complete with races, tug-of-war, and a pie-eating contest, a largest family award (12 children), and a lady's heavyweight contest (winner 218 pounds), then one could be assured that times had indeed changed. The company continued its traditional Christmas treat for youngsters, everything designed to enhance the corporate image. Something new was added, thanks to the strike settlement: the company met with elected representatives of the employees to discuss grievances and other problems.

To instill pride and to increase production, CF&I sponsored contests among its various mines. In December 1921, Crested Butte won in its competitive district, and the local Colorado Supply store ordered 140 hams and forty-six boxes of cigars for the winners. Safety was not sacrificed in these contests. The company concern about safety remained high; the CF&I Safety and Accident Committee searched out ways to prevent accidents and find possible danger points. Other company officials inspected periodically, their visits sometimes including a special social activity such as a dance, movie, or lecture. Colorado Fuel & Iron had become both visible and conscientious by the twenties.

Management continued to add to company housing, building concrete homes in 1920 when rentals became scarce. CF&I carpenters repaired older homes when necessary, and painters brightened them inside and out. That year a standard rental fee of $2 per room per month was charged, with such extras as a sink in the kitchen costing an extra $2; a bathroom, $3; and a basement, $1. With all these facilities, a miner could still rent a four-room house for $14.00 a month. The company would even fence the yard and build a chicken house free of charge. (The latter was a vestige of World War I, when Americans were encouraged to plant gardens and raise their own chickens.)

From CF&I's point of view, company housing was a decided plus, not for the income generated but for easing the housing shortage and raising the morale of the workers. Housing produced greater stability, better living conditions, and, it was hoped, a more contented and cooperative labor force. These eventually translated into higher production and more long-term profits.

For the unmarried miners, CF&I maintained a boarding house, which included quarters for company visitors. Accommodations were more than adequate, and boarders could eat all they wanted in the dining room, with its three large tables loaded with food.

CF&I's degree of involvement leaves little doubt that its Crested Butte operation, including other properties in the area, made a profit for the company. How large is not known, but it was good enough to allow them to buy the land leased from the old Durango Land and Coal in 1918, thereby cutting that tie with the company's history.

One ghost of the past, labor relations, continued to haunt CF&I — though improved since the strike, they had never been completely resolved. A company union emerged from the strike settlement, but the UMW also remained active in Crested Butte. The two factions sparred uneasily back and forth. A slight criticism by the union local in 1920, for instance, regarding safety practices in the Elk Mountain Mine elicited a quick response in the newspaper that the company was in no way at fault, nor had it violated the law in the accident which claimed a miner's life.

On the surface, labor and management relations stayed calm,

but tension heaved underneath, occasionally bursting forth in the form of a strike. As part of a national bituminous miners' strike, Crested Butte miners marched out in November 1919 for higher wages, shorter hours, and "other considerations, not including union recognition." The company came out the winner, without violence, in sharp contrast to what had gone before. This incident was followed in 1921 by a strike to prevent reduction of wages. It, too, ended peacefully, with the miners returning to work at lower wages.

The labor truce was shattered in November 1927 when the miners again walked out, this time shutting down the Big Mine for several months. Trouble had been brewing since the wage reduction two years before. As a result, the Industrial Workers of the World made headway among the men, the more conservative UMW losing out. The IWW brought to Crested Butte a radical, violent image, which did not seem to concern the miners who wanted readdress, something the IWW promised. Sensing trouble building up, the CF&I raised wages in September; the miners now received $.88 per ton in hopes, as the *Gunnison News-Champion* (September 29, 1927) stated, of "definitely killing the bugaboo of an IWW strike."

The ploy failed. The workers demanded a five-day week, minimum scheduled employment days per year, and a six-hour day. The CF&I countered with posters and statements that if the miners went out, the mine would close indefinitely. Neither side gave in and the IWW found new recruits. All the while, its organizers were harassed by the company as much as the law allowed.

The press took the side of the company, calling the IWW organizer, John Perko, a "Red Bolshevik," and the strike illegal. He was thrown in jail for illegally inciting the strike and posting inflammatory notices. That action failed to end the strike and, true to its word, CF&I closed the Big Mine and its other local operations. Active all over Colorado, according to the *Pilot*, IWW strikers closed mines in various districts. The CF&I retaliated locally by threatening to close the Big Mine permanently, claiming that there were already too many mines and too many coal mines in particular. The threat failed to reduce the strikers' ranks, and winter settled in.

With an American flag leading the way, the Crested Butte strikers paraded in November, and then held a rally at which the band played patriotic selections. The production appeared to be designed to show that the strikers were not communists. To raise funds and bolster spirits, dances were held, described by one participant as "jolly affairs." As the strike dragged on, CF&I weakened and in January offered higher wages to tempt the strikers back. The ploy worked in the southern fields, and mines began to reopen after a February vote that called off the strike. The company took a cavalier attitude toward Crested Butte. It seemed in no hurry to settle the dispute, and the wage increase was not in effect in Gunnison County.

The situation had grown increasingly serious; the Denver and Rio Grande Railroad threatened to stop daily train service because of the strike. This perhaps forecast the curtailing or stopping of all trains, which would doom local coal mining. Crested Butte had already lost population because of the strike and faced total collapse if the train stopped running. Gloom and anxiety replaced the earlier friendly, almost happy-go-lucky attitude of the strikers. Crested Butte miners voted to call off the strike in February along with the rest of the state, which prompted the D&RG to rescind its plan to cut services.

Colorado Fuel & Iron held firm, however, and announced that it would be months before the Big Mine opened which it did finally on June 15. Production quickly returned to normal, but 1928 was the only one of the last four years of the 1920s to dip below 100,000 tons of coal produced.

This strike is an interesting one in that, for its duration and seriousness, and considering the track record of the IWW, it was not marked by violence at Crested Butte. This tranquility perhaps confirmed the nature of Crested Butte's miners and general family orientation. Certainly the ethnic fraternal organizations and the Catholic Church tended to mitigate attitudes of violence, and both had a strong following among the immigrant miners and their families.

The role of the IWW is also intriguing. On October 27, 1927, the *Pilot* charged that the "big coal companies" had encouraged IWW organization as a foil to the UMW. If they did do this, they had grabbed a tiger by the tail and were clawed in the process. Once the strike got rolling, CF&I reacted harshly against the outside IWW organizers who tried to hold meetings at Crested Butte. Nonetheless, the

IWW called and maintained the strike before falling to the power of CF&I.

There seems to be no reason to believe that CF&I planned to close the Big Mine permanently — too many years of coal reserves remained. Transportation and declining markets might have made it less profitable, but not to the point of necessitating complete abandonment. The threat appeared to be part of a scheme to force the miners back to work more than anything else. It did not succeed immediately, but it was part of the total pressure that produced the back-to-work vote in February. CF&I could afford to let Crested Butte stew for a while as it concentrated on the more important southern coal field. If necessary, the company could have fared very well without Big Mine production, a fact of life not yet completely comprehended at Crested Butte. Investment there dictated that work continue if at all possible, however. The company did not appreciate the repeated strikes but, as long as coal reserves remained profitable, they would bargain. The 1920s ended as the war years had begun, a decade before, with Crested Butte recovering from another long strike.

Meanwhile, Europe had been teetering on the brink of war for years before finally being engulfed in a titanic conflict. Before it was over the world changed forever and what might be described as the beginning of the modern era dawned. The final crisis started in late July and by August 4, 1914, all the major European powers had become involved. The United States set on the sidelines planning to remain neutral.

The outbreak of war in August 1914 probably concerned few Colorado communities more intimately than Crested Butte. The majority of its residents were immigrants or first generation Americans with close ties to the mother country, which meant eastern Europe, where all the trouble erupted. The *Pilot* provided war coverage, but what took place in the hearts and minds of people during that time cannot be resurrected. The *Pilot* shrewdly laid the blame for the war on Germany, as the United States drew closer to being pulled into it. The Austrian-Hungarian empire remained a silent partner in the conflict, which was profitable thinking on the part of the editor.

Finally, on March 8, 1917, the *Pilot's* editor unequivocally predicted the inevitability of war coming to the United States.

Because of the sacrifice of lives, destruction of property (not forgetting that "murderous, ruthless" submarine which sank ships without warning), and impoverishment of people involved, the writer called war the "greatest calamity" that could come to any nation, but there could be no denying the fact that the demand for high grade steam and hard coal and coke was higher than at any other time in more than twenty years; even metal mining benefited. Perhaps this war boom would finally bring the standard gauge. War-produced business could be exhilarating!

War came as predicted, but not all its benefits were expected by the editor. Coke, as mentioned, never did rebound at Crested Butte. The first local reaction, in April, was a big rush to buy flour and sugar; some stores finally limited the amount that could be purchased, thereby creating shortages and rationing, the fear of which had initially sparked the buying spree. Then came speculation on how many volunteers would respond to Uncle Sam's call; who would be the first to enlist? There was no shortage of volunteers, but within a week men aged twenty-one to thirty were being registered for the draft. The *Pilot* proudly announced that "every person" seemed ready and willing to register.

Some people conjured a threat to the community from resident "traitors," locals whose ties to the motherland proved too strong to be broken by immigration to America. On April 26 the *Pilot* assured foreign-born residents they need not fear an invasion of their personal or property rights as long as they went about their business and conducted themselves in "a law-abiding manner." To be sure the message was clearly comprehended, the paper went on to say, "let it be understood every citizen owes undivided allegiance to the American flag," and that each was expected to fulfill loyally all obligations. Any act, however slight, tending to give aid and comfort to the country's enemies was treason.

Reports of the boys being called up to take physicals were not long in coming. Most passed, but a few suffered damage to their self-images by failing. The next process entailed travel to boot camp, before final transfer to a permanent base. Letters from and news about the "Sammies," as they were called, soon occupied newspaper space. Some came from "over there" and some from such exotic places as Honolulu, about as far from the fighting front as one could get.

Life on the home front geared to meet the war effort. Victory gardens at Crested Butte produced little more than a feeling that the gardener was doing something commendable. More important benefits accrued from money donated to the Red Cross. In June 1917, the men at the Big Mine subscribed a day's wages, and the *Pilot* pleaded for everyone else to join with them and donate. Women could knit, roll bandages, and collect a host of items to help the boys out, thus advancing the war effort and relieving suffering. Everyone could buy liberty bonds. The town was organized for the war effort, as were other American communities, even to the point of having a Smoke Barrel Committee, which sent one of the "fullest and best barrels" of all kinds of tobacco to the Sammies, according to an item in the December *Denver Post*. That was the type of patriotism that could be understood by soldiers and male friends left at home.

When the Italians living on the south side of Crested Butte raised an Italian flag in May 1918, the *Pilot* cheered their patriotism. It seemed only fitting to honor the "splendid and plucky stand" made by the little country against the "German hordes." This was only a sample of the type of journalism readers throughout the country were finding in their favorite papers. Anyone who uttered what could be interpreted as an unpatriotic remark might land in jail, as Mike Tezac did that same month. Before the case dropped from public view, speculation had him confined to one of the internment camps.

As America's involvement in the war entered its second year, it became less exciting and more grim. War, it was found, lacked the anticipated glory. Although the paper did not list any Crested Butte soldier killed in action; Robert Kelley, who grew up there and then moved to California, died in France.

Bond sales in 1918 became more sophisticated and high pressured, even in Crested Butte. Given a quota of $45,000 for the fourth Liberty Loan drive, the town and district patriotically exceeded that, thanks to a well-attended rally at the Princess Theatre which opened with the singing of the "Star-Spangled Banner" and closed with "America."

The joyous news of the armistice, November 11, came at last and was greeted by the clamor of bells, whistles, drums, and guns. All the stores closed, flags of the victorious Allies were strung across Main Street, and everyone had a "hilarious time."

Spontaneous parades, musical concerts, and a huge bonfire entertained the merrymakers when "the war to end all wars" came to its conclusion. "The day will long be remembered by everyone," shouted the *Pilot*.

It is easy to poke fun at the naivety of these people, but they were sincere in their efforts to end the war and firmly believed they had done it and made the world a better place. Just as sincerely, they donated money to help the Red Cross send aid to suffering Europeans and proudly welcomed the veterans home. They also responded to the appeal for "good books" for the boys in hospitals and the troops still stationed in Europe. Once more residents opened their pocketbooks, this time for the Victory Liberty Loan drive. "It was your war, it is your victory. Lend your share to pay the bills."

Now that the German Hun had been vanquished, a new enemy had been found in Bolshevism. The best answer Americans could give to that threat, emphasized the *Pilot*, was to unite behind the Victory Liberty Loan drive. "Bolshevism preys on weakness and vanishes at the first real show of determination to back up principles of real liberty and real government." The intolerance of the war years did not die quickly, nor did the desire for quick, easy solutions to problems.

Crested Butte's difficulties were not confined to political issues. In the late fall and winter of 1918-19, the "Spanish Flu" arrived, part of an international epidemic. The flu was not new — they called it "La Grippe" in the old days — but the severity and deadliness of the most recent virus rated attention. The paper published advice on how to guard against the disease and what to do if one contracted it. Schools were closed in October 1918 to be "on the safe side," and finally quarantine on meetings, travel, and sick people was invoked, all to little avail. Numerous residents became ill and a few died, though not so many here as in some of the other mountain towns. Not until January 1919 was the last quarantine placard removed.

The respite did not last long. A second outbreak flared and finally receded in March; schools reopened and life slowly returned to normal. At its peak, the epidemic put so many in bed that the St. Patrick's dance had only a few couples, a blow to the social calendar. On March 27, the *Pilot* expressed the opinion that Crested Butte should consider itself lucky indeed to have experienced the flu in "so light a form." That opinion did not prevent a few more people from dying.

The flu mitigated the exultation of victory, but once it passed, life appeared to slip back to the old routine. Mere yearnings for an earlier Camelot, however, could not bring back former times. Nostalgia made that prewar period seem like the "good old days" of a simpler, more enjoyable world; the hardships had been forgotten. Better to put aside worries, join the American Legion, and reminisce with one's friends. Together, it was easier to face and accept the approaching changes.

One of those changes, the car, transformed Crested Butte — even CF&I opened a gas station. The automobile, seen occasionally before the war, now became a fact of life. Pressure grew for new and better roads; the *Pilot* called particular attention to the road to Somerset, which had been worked on for ten years and still was not finished before America entered the war. Good roads would also encourage tourism. Crested Butte had promoted tourism for many years without great success, if the register of the Elk Mountain Hotel provided any indication. During a typical summer day from 1915 to 1917 four to six people rented rooms and winter killed even that light traffic. After the war, however, business picked up, and Crested Butte folk took to the road, too, as Phillip Yoklavich and wife did in 1924 when they visited Yellowstone National Park and beyond. By 1927, the *Pilot* mentioned the many tourists in the area throughout the summer.

The automobile was a mixed blessing: it changed dating practices, affected church attendance, made it easier to get to Gunnison to shop, and diminished theater attendance during the summer months. Winter driving habits did not change; cars went back on the blocks and a few locals drove theirs to Salida to be stored until spring returned. This left the train (seasonally) the unchallenged master of transportation, though not for long. With the car came trucks and buses, and with improved winter road maintenance, the train's days were numbered. A portent was the Floresta branch beyond Crested Butte, which was closed and torn up in 1929.

Almost as popular as the car in Crested Butte were movies. They helped to break down the isolation barrier. Newsreels and features brought the outside world to this valley as never before. No longer need there be any kind of communication or cultural isolation. The latest fads and styles quickly became familiar to the coal miner and his wife. For a brief time the town had hopes of becoming a movie producing center. In 1920, the Artograph Film Company sent representatives to check out the area's landscape and, according to the *Pilot*, they "went wild over our lakes and scenery" and saw the snow as a fine background for moving pictures. They promised to return in the spring with actors, a promise never kept.

Rivaling movies in popularity was the radio, which arrived in the early 1920s with cracking, hissing, and a faint voice from somewhere out there beyond the Elk Mountains. Though only two radio sets existed in town in January 1923, a radio club was organized. People invited friends to come over to listen. To hear canaries singing from Los Angeles seemed like a miracle to the editor of the *Pilot*, who also heard music from Fort Worth, Denver, Kansas City, and Scoby, Oklahoma, that same evening.

As these new forms of communication attracted attention and popularity, interest in the local newspaper declined. Gunnison people purchased it in 1917, hired a local editor, and did the printing in a more modern plant at the county seat. This procedure worked well initially — the old equipment in the *Pilot* office had seen long service — but the inevitable happened. The local correspondent or editor was allowed a column or two of Crested Butte news, and the rest was all about Gunnison, the state, or the nation. A local newspaper could not be maintained without this arrangement, and the spark went out of local news. The excitement of earlier journalism evaporated, emphasizing that Crested Butte was no longer the town it once had been.

Another change in the twenties resulted from a holdover of the crusading zeal of a decade before, the one that produced prohibition. If the town "[had gone] dry gently and peacefully as Mary's little lamb" on January 1, 1916, it had not stayed that way. The car greatly facilitated bootlegging. Revenue agents and the county sheriff soon arrived on the scene but had little luck in finding the bootleggers and their elusive stills. By the twenties their shenanigans had become a game, one suspected bootlegger being so bold as to announce that parties on "my trail for bootlegging" would always find him at the Smith Hill Boarding House. The dauntless sheriff and agents kept at their raiding, arresting a few people in the process. What good they did is questionable. In 1923 the *Pilot* announced the recent arrival of three carloads of grapes and described the ensuing "happy-go-lucky" smiles on many faces.

Finally, in October 1927, success crowned the "Feds'" efforts. They arrested nine suspects "caught with the goods," and destroyed a few stills, the largest having a fifty-gallon capacity. The *Pilot* felt sure someone had tipped off "our most prominent bootleggers," who never seemed to be caught with the "hooch." Thus did another great reform idea go the way of other moral crusades, such as the one to make the world safe for democracy.

Enforcement of prohibition was the longest-lived criminal issue in Crested Butte, which did not otherwise wink at law violations. Drunkenness persisted as its usual troublesome self, enhanced by the general attitude toward bootlegging. In addition there were the petty nuisances, such as boys cutting clothes lines and too many dogs wandering around. To cure this latter problem, some people took the solution into their own hands and scattered poison. The *Pilot* scolded that the "measly cur" who did that ought to be found dead alongside one of the victims. Some exotic crimes occasionally surfaced, as when the sheriff arrested Rada Novak for having a wife in the old country and one in Crested Butte. Interestingly, the Ku Klux Klan apparently made little headway here during the Klan-dominated Colorado of the mid-twenties. The *Pilot* had been opposed to it as early as 1922, and the predominance of Catholics guaranteed it would have a small audience for its bigotry and hate.

City government was routine, once the socialist threat was decisively repelled in 1915. The major issue over the years remained economy in government, which seems to have aroused what little interest there was in some elections. To have only one ticket on the ballot was not unusual now. Names of the trustees revealed both northern and eastern European origins — another barrier had fallen before the new immigrant.

"Some old, some new" might serve as an appropriate caption for the 1920s. When the Rev. F.A. Hatch of Pueblo could openly announce talks on sex education with slides, then times had decidedly changed. To be sure, the afternoon lecture was reserved for ladies and the evening one for men and boys — no mixing of the sexes with this issue. The moral prudishness of the previous generation gave way to the more permissive roaring twenties. For the first time, going on to college became an opportunity for more than just the few upper-class children. Most went to Western State in Gunnison, a few as far away as the University of Colorado in Boulder. Football challenged baseball for interest among the sporting crowd, particularly now that one could jump in a car and drive to Gunnison for a Saturday afternoon college game. Hip flasks, raccoon coats, and Joe College invaded Crested Butte!

Some old familiar things remained to provide anchors amid the changes of the twenties. The public schools, a pride of the community, were doing a fine job. Expansion came in 1916 when the ninth and tenth grades were added. Six years later the next two grades followed, thus completing the high school curriculum. These additions necessitated another building, which was completed in 1927. Until these years, anyone wishing to go to high school had to board out at Gunnison; Crested Butte had finally come of age in the field of education.

Teaching continued to be the special province of women, who remained dedicated even without equal pay for equal work. For instance, during the 1922-23 school year, the top male teacher received $1,850; the top woman, $1,125. Men also attained the title "professor;" women did not. The liberation of the twenties took a while to reach the Elk Mountains! For years the local schools' primary responsibility had been what county superintendent of schools, Luella Johnson, so succinctly stated in 1916: "Their great duty is to make citizens of the children who come from across the sea." This they had done, taking over the task CF&I had originally started for the parents. The company, incidentally, did not involve itself in school matters, except for occasional special lectures and financial support.

School life in Crested Butte was much like that of its contemporaries elsewhere. In 1920, after several youngsters were injured by snowballs, snowballing was prohibited near the buildings. That same year, a diphtheria scare reduced attendance for nearly a month until the crisis passed; whooping cough and other epidemic illnesses did the same thing. The *Pilot* encouraged parental visits to the school in the belief that they would increase interest and allow parents to find out how their children were performing. When the third through sixth grades won second prize in a National Health Crusade tournament in 1924, the newspaper and a proud community applauded them.

That second community pillar, the church, also provided continuity amid the onslaught of change. The Union Congregational retained its position as the Protestant center, finally being able to support a full-time minister for a short while in the 1920s. Its success proved more illusory than substantive; St. Patrick's Catholic Church had become by far the larger and more popular. Union Congregational's Mrs. Addie Decker observed in 1917, during one of those periods when her church could not afford a pastor, that the foreign population made it necessary to rely on the Home Mission Society to supply the pulpit, because Crested Butte's present large majority was non-English speaking Roman Catholic. With a trace of bitterness, she, nevertheless, hit the fundamental religious truth of the first half of the twentieth century.

In contrast, St. Patrick's, with its 500 or so members, was one of the region's largest churches, and a resident priest conducted services. It had been a vital force in the community for nearly a generation now and would continue to be through the end of the coal mining era.

The same Slavic peoples who supported the Catholic church also ardently joined their ethnic lodges, which flourished before and after the war. The cohesiveness these organizations provided continued to shelter the immigrant from the strange world around him and gave a social outlet second to none. The fact that they offered various types of insurance policies enhanced their attraction for people who could not obtain or did not know how to secure one in other ways.

These aliens still found themselves segregated to some degree in a community they dominated. Slavs, for example, crowded boarding houses run by their own; managing a boarding house afforded a great opportunity for their women to gain an economic foothold. Margaret Golobich commented that she always looked at a prospective boarder's hand to see if his "ruke" was roughened from work (no definition of ruke was provided). If not, he was turned away. Michele Veltri clearly summed up these immigrants' contribution to Crested Butte in an honors paper at Western State College in 1972. In the final analysis, she wrote, perhaps the greatest memorial for these people would be their fun-loving industriousness, strength in the face of hardships, and their painfully neat homes and gardens.

The CF&I encouraged those gardens by judging lawns, gardens, and flowers and awarding prizes to the best. Agriculture and ranching retained their precarious hold in the area; farmers and ranchers, however, continued working at the mines in the winter to supplement their incomes. One of the most eagerly awaited times of the year was the day the trucks came from Somerset and beyond (over the finally finished road) to bring fresh fruits and vegetables raised in that garden spot of the Western Slope.

Life at Crested Butte continued to revolve around the Big Mine, but the *Pilot*'s local column (August 1922) recounted other events, such as the Republican delegates motoring to Gunnison, a family reunion for the Kerrs and Rosses, the death of a former resident in a Telluride mine accident, and the fire department's putting out a slight blaze on the roof of the Niccoli house. That last item put into perspective a frustrated volunteer fireman's remark that "we've never saved a building, but we always save the lot." Visitors came and went. The local penchant for dances never waned, although the Charleston and Black Bottom lacked the grace of the popular waltz of a generation before. The polka had not lost in favor. Babies' births were announced, illnesses were recounted, and it was noted that the movie at the Princess Theatre was unusually good. A new lessee of the Elk Mountain Hotel promised to renovate and improve the place. By October it advertised a complete fried chicken dinner, "from soups to nuts," for $.75. The town's cement walk had been extended, which was "very nice for the people living in the lower end of town."

Labor Day, the most important communitywide holiday, sometimes turned out to be a "miserably cold day." Armistice Day reminded everyone of the sacrifices of the war, as did "Forget-Me-Not-Day," sponsored by the Disabled American Veterans. Christmas was still the favorite of the young and the young-at-heart. It wouldn't have been Halloween without a prank or two; old-timers fondly remembered that night. Fritz Kochevar and a group of friends found that by climbing on each others' backs they could reach the street lights and unscrew them. This they continued to do until one of the extra deputies, hired especially for that evening, put a stop to the practice.

"None of this home at 9:00 stuff," recalled John Panian. "Dancing, or getting a bottle of wine and the buggy, and staying out till at *least* 5:00 in the morning. That was the way to do it. Have fun!" A skating rink opened in 1927, with skaters gliding to the music of the Merry-Makers Orchestra. No one had to feel deprived by a lack of social opportunities — Crested Butte offered everything from Camp Fire Girls and Boy Scouts to a Ladies' Social Club and Lyceum series.

Main Street businesses showed the changing times; as the twenties slipped away, the number of stores declined. Mail order business and the easy access the car provided to Gunnison cut into the local market. It would seem likely also that the Colorado Supply Company's advantageous position took a toll of some of its weaker competitors. Traveling specialists supplemented local businesses. One of them was Irene Ramsey, who came up from Gunnison to give permanent waves to the ladies.

If the CF&I company store hurt business, the company's building of more homes in 1920 relieved a housing shortage that at its worst saw as many as three families crowding into one house. Colorado Fuel & Iron's continued presence brought both good and bad to Crested Butte.

Nothing could be done about the harsh, capricious weather. A frost in July 1924 ruined the gardens, and the hard winters took their toll, just as they had done back in the eighties. Residents had to be reminded to clean up in the spring: "Make the town as clean as possible, and its reputation will be all the better." Even with improved medicines over the years, Crested Butte folks still suffered from all those ailments, real and imaginary, that cursed an earlier generation — backaches, colds, palpitation of the heart, female troubles, sensitive skin, and gray hair. A multitude of patent medicines promised relief, although the Pure Food and Drug Law was hot on their trail.

In the midst of the changes of the roaring twenties, a strong yearning for the past was evidenced most graphically by the twenty, thirty, and forty years ago column in the paper. The history of Crested Butte held a fascination for the readers. Letters from old timers highlighted some issues, retired *Pilot's* editor John Phillips being the most prolific with his reminiscences. Those "stirring days" appeared as a different world to the reader, one to which he had not been partner. Obituaries of those pioneers also received careful attention. Hardly varying, they praised the individual's sterling qualities, friendly nature, and success. No failures seemed to have occurred. Perhaps the unfortunates were simply ignored — or else they drifted completely out of Crested Butte's orbit.

As 1929 sped toward 1930, the future of Crested Butte never looked better. An editorial in the *Elk Mountain Pilot* (October 24) praised CF&I for deciding to electrify the Big Mine, ensuring a great future for Gunnison County's largest industrial center. The author concluded that when the future of a community the size and importance of Crested Butte brightened, the whole county would immediately benefit: that promised prosperity was at hand.

Crested Butte, 1900-1920:

A Photographic Essay

Crested Butte was a coal town during these decades and proud of it; there were no marked changes in appearance, except where the Colorado Fuel and Iron made some additions. The significant change occurred in the makeup of the population; the eastern European immigrant came to claim this community as almost entirely his own.

The frontier atmosphere evaporated over the years, and Crested Butte emerged to become like many other isolated mountain towns, engaged in a struggle for an existence based upon mining. It was never a typical company town, and its inhabitants had more freedom and opportunity than were allotted to many of their contemporaries in the coal mining districts.

The view of Crested Butte from the Big Mine about 1910. Second Street crosses the tracks, taking the miners to and from work.

Colorado Fuel, Iron & Steel

On this 1909 day, the Big Mine works at full capacity. Production of over 125,000 tons that year made it Colorado's fifth ranked coal mine.

United States Geological Survey

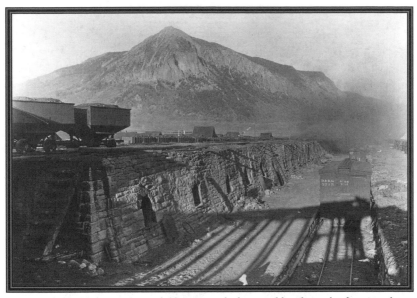

If the wind should change, the wash blowing on the line would no longer be clean. Coal cars brought the coal to the ovens, railroad cars took the coke to market. The product of bituminous coal, coke was heated to drive off coal's volatile components.
George Beam, photographer—Jackson Thode Collection

The unsung heroes of Crested Butte coal mining were the mules that hauled the cars. Here some of them graze in the corral outside the mule barn.
Colorado Fuel, Iron & Steel

Near the end of an era, the Big Mine on a wintry April morning in 1951. It operated another year before closing.

Colorado Fuel, Iron & Steel

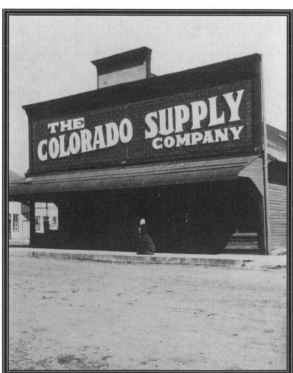

The Colorado Supply store was the oldest and most obvious example of CF&I activity in the community, although business appears to be slow on this fall day.
Colorado Fuel, Iron & Steel

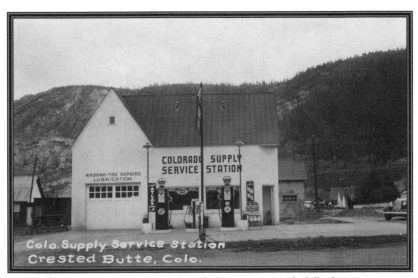

CF&I had an impact on the community aside from its mine on the hill. The company changed with the times and introduced a service station when cars and trucks increased in popularity.

Colorado Fuel, Iron & Steel

CF&I met the demand for housing with these homes, which tended to give Crested Butte the appearance of a company town.

Colorado Fuel, Iron & Steel

In the twentieth century, as well as the nineteenth, the Denver and Rio Grande held the key to successful coal mining and Crested Butte's future. Engine No. 32 and tender pose, probably on their way to pick up coal cars.

Jackson Thode

In 1926, and every other winter, the D&RG battled snow. This rotary plow struggles to clear the tracks.

Fred Vernon

Resplendent in bright uniforms, the band—and some young fans—stand proudly for a photograph. This is perhaps the Crested Butte Cornet Band, which flourished in the early 1900s. It played at concerts, parades, and other social events.

Amon Carter Museum

The site of many a social gathering and council meeting, the City Hall attracts only a stray dog at this moment.

Colorado Fuel, Iron & Steel

Some of the boys standing in front of a local saloon. Depending on one's persuasion, these establishments either provided a home away from home or an enticing gateway to hell.
Amon Carter Museum

Crested Butte at its mining peak.

U.S. Geological Survey

There may have been joy in Crested Butte this day as the local nine took on a rival. The number of automobiles suggests the 1920s.

Amon Carter Museum

The Ruby-Anthracite Mine at Floresta in 1909.

U.S. Geological Survey

Snow, sled, and warm clothes, what could be more perfect?

Author

A boy and his dog add up to fun.

Author

Skiing equipment and dress in the late nineteenth and early twentieth centuries were far cries from that of today. Crested Butte was also decades away from being a skiing mecca.
Amon Carter Museum

Elk Avenue looks peaceful in the early 1950s, almost like a ghost town street. The coal mining era had come to a close; Crested Butte awaited a new start.
Amon Carter Museum

CHAPTER 6
Twilight of an Era
1930-1945

On Thursday, October 24, 1929, the American stock market, considered a bellwether of 1920s prosperity, collapsed under a frenzy of selling. The shock vibrated throughout the whole country, triggering the worst depression in the nation's history, one which would last for a decade.

Out in Crested Butte, the stock market collapse created interest but was not particularly worrisome to most, since they lacked the wherewithal to indulge in stock speculation. While most of the rest of the country endured the horrors of economic collapse, Crested Butte seemed to live a charmed life. Although Colorado showed an overall decline of twenty percent in coal production because of the depression and more extensive use of oil and gas, the Big Mine increased production thirty-four percent to 150,805 tons, the best in twenty-five years. Electrification of the mine was completed and new pit cars, mining machines, and locomotives were introduced at a cost of $85,000. Arthur Roeder, president of CF&I, expressed the pride of the company and community in the mine when he commented in August 1930, "[the] Crested Butte mine is a remarkable property and we anticipate steady production in that field for many years to come. The dawn of a much brighter day in coal mining is at hand."

Seldom had circumstances in Crested Butte been more san-guine than in that year. A convivial organization, calling itself the "prospective bridegroom union," honored its ex-members and brides after they took the leap into matrimony. Large crowds cheered local favorite John Nemanic to a two-fall vic-tory in the western Colorado wrestling championship, a tri-umph for the community as well. The Crested Butte Game and Fish Protective Association stocked local streams and lakes and erected a campground in anticipation of the many tourists expected. The fact that they did not materialize was the only shadow on that year.

The good times and steady production carried on into the spring of 1931. But Friday, April 23, brought an end to Crested Butte's charmed existence. The blow came from an unexpected quarter — Charles Ross, the leading local entrepreneur of the past decade and a long-time resident, failed in his striving to achieve success. That a businessman should stumble was not in itself unusual; the same thing had happened to many others before him. Ross, however, took the bank with him.

Pennsylvania-born Ross lived in Crested Butte at least as early as 1885, when the census taker recorded his father, moth-er, sister, and six-year-old Charles. A dynamic and forceful man, Ross soon made his mark. At various times he held municipal office, worked on the newspaper, led the Republicans as county chairman, was an active Mason, served as secretary to the light and water company, and owned the movie theater. He became cashier of the bank, then the bank's vice president and director, and president of the Ross Coal Company, which eventually became the Columbine Anthracite Company. Here was a man to be admired, praised, and emulated. Ross had achieved success as defined by the business world of Crested Butte and become a pillar of the community.

The bank had weathered several brief crises before and, with Ross and the equally well-known Dr. John Rockefeller as presi-dent, it seemed to offer a safe depository with no risk. That con-fidence made the shock worse when the doors closed on April 23. How could such a thing happen? Many hard-earned miners' dollars were deposited there, and none of them was insured. The *Pilot* understated the situation when it reported that the closing "caused quite a commotion." The majority of the community's residents stood to lose their life's savings unless the bank reopened, and businessmen depended on its operation.

Rumors, both good and bad, whipped the stunned town. The *Pilot* on April 30 could say only: "It is hoped by all that this dark cloud of misfortune which has hit our peaceful community may have a silver lining and a bright future still in store for all." Similar optimism had evaporated elsewhere in the country in 1929-30, plunging Americans into even greater gloom.

Immediate repercussions hit when the light and water company announced it was cutting back on electricity because of the bank's closing. The American Red Cross formulated lists of families left practically destitute by the "financial calamity." Now people began to understand what the depression really meant. To make matters worse, the Big Mine was temporarily shut down; when CF&I announced its reopening May 1, it provided the only good news in a black week.

Hardly had the bank's doors closed when speculation about the reasons became rampant. One answer came from the cashier, Victor Benson, who also happened to be the mayor, when he confessed to making false entries to meet the payrolls of the Columbine Anthracite Company against presumed deposits in Denver. He was instantly sentenced to six years in prison in Canon City. The *Pilot* considered such speed remarkable in the annals of the district court. Charges against Benson had actually been filed on April 7, helping to bring about the closing. State bank examiners and the district attorney's office then sifted through the bank's records to see what else had occurred.

No one knew exactly how much the deficit would be; it started at $31,000 and rose alarmingly as the days went by. Almost everybody felt sorry for Dr. Rockefeller, eighty-two years old and a long time Crested Butte benefactor — it just did not seem fair to have his career end on this dismal note. As president of the bank he received some blame for its demise, along with a great deal of sympathy as a major bank depositor. The town itself lost $4,900 of its general fund and $2,600 of the light and water fund on deposit in the bank.

By mid-May the deficit reached $100,000, and the scope of the calamity was becoming obvious. Ross, who lived in Denver now, was arrested for alleged involvement in fraudulent activities related to the bank's operation. Reportedly ill, he refused comment except to say lamely that he had not been at Crested Butte in a "long time" and did not know a thing about the situation there.

The bank did not reopen; it never would. The only question at issue was what percentage of their money the depositors might recover, which depended solely on the assets that could be liquidated. The bank examiner worked to untangle the mess, while the district attorney prepared charges against Ross. Crested Butte merely watched and waited. One of the first moves by the bank's receiver was a foreclosure suit against the Columbine Anthracite Company and the appointment of a receiver to insure its early reopening. Judgments against the mine and company totaled about $40,000; if that money could be recovered, the bank's position would be strengthened.

As the months passed, Ross's health deteriorated swiftly because of his heart condition. Considering the calamity he had helped to create, it was remarkable that Ross's many friends, on hearing he had been taken quite seriously ill, wished him a speedy recovery (*Pilot*, August 6, 1931). It showed, apparently, the respect still held for him. Some elation came that same month when the bank's receiver announced a ten percent dividend on deposits; even that "small amount of ready cash" brought joy to the community.

A year went by with no further dividends forthcoming, nor had Ross been brought into court. When the trial finally got underway, it became obvious that the bank had fallen into a tangled morass largely because of its dealing with the Columbine Anthracite Company. Ross had been involved in both enterprises and in September 1932 was found guilty of embezzlement. His lawyer promptly argued for a new trial, while his client languished in the Gunnison jail. Then, in December, the inevitable happened — Ross died from his heart condition. Considering the pressure he had been under the past sixteen months, it was remarkable he had lived that long.

In death, Charles Ross partly redeemed himself and helped clear up the financial chaos he had created in the community. He left a $75,000 life insurance policy to the Columbine Anthracite Company, which could now repay the bank and put the mine in a position to resume operation. The previous summer, Ross had insisted that his insurance be kept in force, although the major bondholders of the bank wanted at that time to surrender it for its cash value of approximately $7,000. The policy was paid out and hopes for more dividends were kept alive.

A 20 percent dividend came in March 1933; it was, according to the *Pilot* of March 2, not a real dividend, which was true.

> *Nevertheless, it will be very welcome to a couple of hundred Crested Butte citizens. They have already received two ten percent payments and there is a possibility of ten to twenty percent more at some future date.*

Other dividends followed, augmented by an auction of items belonging to the Bank of Crested Butte, some land holdings in particular. Not until January 1938 was the eighth and final repayment made, bringing the total to 78.5 percent returned to the depositors on their accounts. This closed the book on the failure of a bank and one man's entrepreneur dream. As a Crested Butte resident later said, the bank's failure was a worse blow to the town than the final closing of the mines. In a day when times were generally bad throughout the country, having this happen when it did plummeted Crested Butte into an emotional and economic depression. As with Ross, Mayor Victor Benson received surprisingly little personal blame. After his release from prison, he motored up from Gunnison one April day in 1934 and enjoyed a visit with old friends. The attitude seemed to have been that a well-intentioned error in judgment had kept the mine going on the assumption that production would allow repayments of the notes. Certainly Ross showed the best of intentions with his insurance policy, and he had done a great deal to help Crested Butte before the bank and mine crisis of 1929-1931.

Although the depression had not initially affected the Big Mine, it did hurt the smaller local mines, whose precarious existence was threatened further by the bank failure. Most closed, and the rest reduced their work week. The years 1931 and 1932 were hard ones for all; even the Big Mine shut down for repairs, and the Crested Butte district suffered. The Big Mine rebounded and, in 1933, entered an extended period of high production. The others were not so fortunate, reopening and closing periodically. This instability hurt the district and made it all the more reliant on CF&I.

For those miners who could find work (and CF&I employed over 200 men by the mid-1930s) times got better. For example, Johnny Somrak, whose father had been killed in the mine in 1923, went to work in the Big Mine in August 1932. This 110-pound, seventeen-year-old mined to help support his family of nine. He remembered:

> *I went to work — 9 hour work day — no time off for lunch, eat it whenever you could get a bite or maybe never. Everything was on the fly. The wage was $2.97 per day. [Underground wages were $4.44 per day or about $.40 or $.44 a ton contract tonnage.]*

> *They put me to work with 3 guys that weighed 180 to 200 pounds each, young fellows. The first 2 weeks they about killed me off, but I made up my mind to do it, or die. Well I got toughened out and I made it. My take home pay for 5 days would only be about $12.00 a week after taking off bathhouse rental, hospital, medical insurance, etc. As the years went on conditions improved very much. We had some good working periods and some slack no work times during the summer — shutdown for 60 to 90 days at a time — no demand for coal. Then we would go to work wherever a dollar could be picked up.*

The *Pilot* (February 13, 1936) observed that, although the law allowed miners to work only thirty-five hours per week, a coal shortage permitted officials to authorize a six-day week, which reminded the correspondent of "the good old days" before the depression swept the country. One discouraging aspect of the job, however, was reminiscent of an earlier time. Regarding the role of foreman and superintendent, Somrak commented, "If you were in with the mine foreman and others underground you had it made. If not, you worked damn hard and very little pay. The company bosses all had their favorite bosses' pets, like school teachers." John Krizmanich and Whitey Sporcich concurred that the foremen were particularly oppressive.

The depression dragged on, but times were getting better. Superintendent H.D. Pinkney announced in July 1937 that "our men have worked longer during the past fiscal year than for many years." He was not whistling in the dark; for the calendar year 1937 the Big Mine topped 280,000 tons, at that time the second largest production in its history.

This achievement came along with the final victory of the United Mine Workers in their struggle to represent the CF&I miners. Pressure built against the so-called Rockefeller plan (company union), and with the national victory of the labor-oriented Democrats in 1932 and the subsequent New Deal, labor received a tremendous boost. As a result, CF&I found itself unable to maintain its plan, and the workers were given the opportunity to vote on the question. The results were foregone. The Big Mine crew voted 166 against, 38 for, a ratio nearly duplicated by the final total Colorado vote. In December 1933 CF&I signed a contract with the United Mine Workers of America, and the Crested Butte local gained new respectability. One of the first tangible results was the local election of the check weighmaster at the Big Mine.

This, of course, put new spice into the labor pot — a national strike could pull the Crested Butte miners out along with all the rest. They were still only small fish in a very large pond dominated by the eastern locals. A 1935 strike was averted by President Franklin Roosevelt's intervention and by ratification of a new national contract. The UMW's president, John L. Lewis, one of the most outspoken labor leaders of his generation, led the union into a strong bargaining position, much stronger than CF&I could withstand.

The impact of the national organization was demonstrated in April 1941, when Lewis called the miners out after a failure in negotiations. Crested Butte's 280 miners walked out, too, and as a result idled the train crews on the local line. The strike was settled in ten days, but the Big Mine stayed closed for three weeks.

Under the union's watchful eye and with continued vigilance by the company, safety was stressed at the Big Mine. For example, all employees wore goggles, special classes, including first aid, were taught, and examinations were conducted on safety procedures in coal mining. Diplomas were awarded to those who passed. The Colorado Fuel & Iron mine rescue crew gained local renown and was called out to other nearby mines in emergencies. When a fatal accident did occur, something that could never be completely eliminated, lessons were learned. The state coal inspector praised the Big Mine for very good discipline after investigating the death of Louis Chiodo in December 1933. Any miner or employee who violated mining laws or safety rules was punished by being discharged or laid off for several days — Chiodo had violated both and paid the supreme price. CF&I showed its concern by deferring daily operation until after the funeral.

Its coal mining past continued to haunt Crested Butte. Well-known old-time resident Henderson Fawcett revisited the town in the summer of 1938 and discussed with the *Pilot*'s correspondent the Jokerville explosion in which his father and brother died. Eight men were killed in the Big Mine from 1930 through 1940, one price for the increased production of those years. Nonfatal accidents were much more common. Sometimes they ran in cycles, as in January 1940, when local miners fell victim to smashed fingers, broken foot bones, and a collision with a mule.

Coal mining reigned as undisputed king, but hard-rock mining issued another challenge. One of the things Roosevelt's New Deal did to improve the economy was to raise the price of gold to $35 an ounce. With jobs scarce or nonexistent, panning for gold seemed a likely way to make ends meet. Back to the Elk Mountains came the prospectors; others, not so skillful, took classes in Denver on panning and mining before launching out on their own. Washington Gulch had not seen so much activity in years, as placers and lode claims merited renewed interest. For a couple of summer seasons, the area hummed with activity. Then, when jobs became more plentiful and the economic situation brightened, placer and hard-rock mining tailed off. Finally, quiet returned once more; the old days had not been revived.

More than ever now Crested Butte depended on its coal mine. Tourism dropped off, agriculture was depressed, hard-rock mining never amounted to much, and no other alternative offered economic relief. Only incurable optimists could have said that Crested Butte was anything more than a coal town.

After the bank failure, depression descended on the community with a vengeance. What had been a normal, if somewhat slower, economy now ground nearly to a halt. People who in the 1920s envisioned America as the land of opportunity, where there was "no such thing as no chance," lost that vision of their country and themselves. America had become a different place in those dark days, steering toward an uncertain future.

Abundant signs of change were evident. In the late twenties hardly an issue of the *Pilot* did not comment about someone undergoing surgery. Suddenly, with the hard times, operations nearly ceased, leaving one to conclude that either the locals amazingly achieved better health or they did not have the money for medical expenses. Cattle stealing proliferated alarmingly, along with illegal siphoning of gasoline. The *Pilot* concluded in September 1931, "Great is temptation in these hard times." The receiver of the Peanut Mine, Judge Clifford Stone, placed the times in proper perspective: "However, conditions in the country are unusual, and we cannot predict how long steady work will continue. We hope to relieve the distressing situation among many of the families of Crested Butte and will operate the mine as long as possible." In spite of his assurances, the Peanut operated only spasmodically.

Some kept a stiff upper lip and tried to muddle through; a "cheer-up" dance at the time of the bank failure illustrated their efforts. But the slump worsened and happy days appeared to be gone forever. Then came Christmas, 1931 — toys and presents were few and far between under the tree. The day was spent "rather quietly in our community," the paper observed, with enough snow on the ground to make it seem like a real Christmas. A Christmas evening dance to benefit the Catholic Church brightened the holiday somewhat and reportedly was a "grand success."

Times did not improve much in 1932, an election year. Crested Butte, Gunnison County, Colorado, and the rest of the United States showed what they thought of President Herbert Hoover and the Republicans by voting strongly for the Democrats. They also voted to scrap Colorado prohibition, which had never worked well anyway. Interest in the election personalities and issues brought out record numbers of voters.

The election put in office President Franklin Roosevelt and his (at the moment) vaguely defined New Deal program. "Try something, and if it does not work, try something else" became the motto of the federal government's efforts to restore the economy and the people's faith in themselves. When it finally got into high gear, the New Deal provided a sweeping program of relief, recovery, and reform. For Crested Butte this meant $7,200 for water works improvements, which translated into jobs for local men. It meant an adult school program for the unemployed or partly employed, taught by teachers on relief. Direct federal relief came as early as the spring of 1933, followed by the popular Civilian Conservation Corps camps, highway construction funds, and a reforestation program that hired only people on relief. It produced jobs such as snow shoveling by Works Progress Administration workers and spawned a host of New Deal agencies, lovingly called the scrambled alphabet.

The New Deal worked at Crested Butte; it supported the community through those depression days until the Big Mine resumed full-scale operations and a few of the smaller mines reopened. Only then, when the grimmest days were diminishing, could Crested Butte stage "depression parties." The guests dressed to represent hard times, something they would have been embarrassed to do during the darkest days.

Perhaps the most lasting improvements to come to Crested Butte as part of the New Deal package were the REA power lines and finally, a steady electrical supply. The failure of the bank and the 1934 drought, which threatened the plant's water supply, had demonstrated the vulnerability of the electric company and its undependability. By 1938 prospects were good for receiving REA connections, a thought that cheered both residents and council members. In December 1941 those connections were made at last, and the old light and water company passed into history. Service, power, and reliability quickly improved — Crested Butte could modernize along with the rest of the country!

With the New Deal came more federal intervention into community and individual lives, not an onerous trade-off, since it pulled the community out of the depression of '31. CF&I still played the largest role, even with Uncle Sam's inroads. The company sent over painters and carpenters in the spring to repair and spruce up its houses, and officials gave "interesting talks" before school assemblies and general audiences. It sponsored a home safety club and program, the company physician treated his patients, and CF&I purchased hay and grain which helped local farmers. The CF&I Hotel, with its "clean, comfortable rooms, good meals and reasonable prices," served miners and visitors. On Main Street no business rivaled the Colorado Supply Company, which had the misfortune of burning again in January 1937. It took ten months, but CF&I opened another (using the old storehouse as temporary quarters), which was hailed as a model industrial store, the finest on the Western Slope. The new store lived up to those claims, containing departments for meats, groceries, dry goods, bakery, and babies' needs, among other things, with room in the basement to store ten cars and supplies.

Community life returned to a more normal pace in the mid-thirties. The ever popular dances continued, allowing couples a chance to forget everything but the music and companionship of friends around them. One of the enduring strengths of Crested Butte continued to be the town's close-knit nature: people pulling together. As several old-timers commented, "The town seemed to realize that if they didn't pull together, it would be very tough."

Efforts to clean up the town continued each spring, with the usual varied results. School years came and went with some innovations. The first high school band, attired in yellow capes with purple trim and white shirts and trousers, made its debut in 1936-37, to the cheers of proud parents and the *Pilot*. The PTA involved parents more in the life of the school; they worked on various projects that included purchasing books for the library. A milestone of sorts was reached when the high school alumni club was organized in 1933, with its not-too-old members enjoying a card party and "appetizing" refreshments. Like many others, the school suffered financial hard times in the early 1930s, forcing a budget cut and reduction of services as a last resort. The New Deal and general economic improvement hastened its recovery.

Alvene Eppich Dalla, who taught at Crested Butte from 1937 to 1940, recalled how the times affected her when the teachers were paid in warrants: "You know how they are — if you cash them in, you take a discount, but if you can hold them until the money comes in, then you can make money on them." She remembered that people reached out to help each other. "Some of the old people thought the teachers weren't getting paid, so they would send gifts, canned goods, home canned goods, and different kinds of things for the teachers. They were very generous people, they were very kind in that respect."

When she began her career in Crested Butte, Alvene was paid $1,200 a year to teach fourth grade. Finding an apartment presented a problem for the single women teachers (married

women, apparently, were not hired), until the school board finally built a "teacherage" large enough for four people. There was an
unwritten rule at the time that half the teachers be Catholic and
half Protestant. Alvene said:

> *The parents never interfered with school, but they wanted*
> *strict discipline. Teaching was no problem at all — you could*
> *put across anything you wanted. You could teach all day*
> *long and never have a discipline problem, because if word*
> *ever got back to the parents, the child would get doubly dis-*
> *ciplined when he got home.*
>
> *We never heard a word from CF&I. We never heard a word;*
> *they never interfered in any way.*
>
> *The parents saw to it [children's homework and learning],*
> *and because of that they advanced very well. They did not*
> *pass a child just because he wanted to be with his peers. I*
> *had some very good students. I did have some slow learners.*

She had fun with her students, especially one winter when they
built an igloo in the schoolyard. "It was great fun with the kids.
They were all energetic, they were all interested."

Dalla's introduction to the community included the joke
played on all newcomers — the one about the two-story out-
house (necessary because of the deep snow). As an outsider,
however, she saw Crested Butte in transition between the old
and the new:

> *The town as a whole was different. You felt so different when*
> *you got from there into Gunnison. They lived among them-*
> *selves, and this was the way it was and this was the way*
> *they liked it. They carried over old country traditions, and*
> *they lived that way. They taught their young people, more or*
> *less. And the young people, when they had children, they*
> *became more modern, more worldly educated.*
>
> *In a way they were sort of a superstitious people. One day*
> *the mine was working, but we teachers were off for some hol-*
> *iday or another. Three of us decided that we would walk to*

the mine and see what was up there. Well, as we neared the mine, they said, 'You cannot come any closer, because women in or near the mine would induce an accident.' That was it — we could not come any closer. We had to turn around and go back.

She also remembered that the town was run by "sort of a silent ruler." "You knew it, it was just word of mouth. You did what he said. That's all there was to it." His name and position have, unfortunately, been lost to history. Looking back from the vantage point of over forty years, Elvene Dalla closed by praising those "wonderfully kind, sympathetic, generous people" who made her three years so enjoyable.

Casual visitors to Crested Butte did not sense the town's special qualities; they saw it only briefly and from a different perspective. Maurice Hayden liked the local fishing so much he traveled up from Pueblo several times to try his luck. But there was "not much to do at night; we spent most of our time in beer joints." Anne Simpson was there for the New Year's Eve dance in 1939: "That dance was something else; boy, did they whirl around. It was quite a new experience to me. It was really something to meet those foreign people and see how they danced and how effervescent they were, just having the best time of their lives." Regarding the town, however, Simpson pictured it as "old, but clean," while Hayden graphically described it as a "little one-horse town."

The late 1930s economic revival reactivated the dormant efforts to entice tourists. Fishing, hunting, and scenic drives were touted, and winter sports – tobogganing and skiing – were subjects of renewed promotion. By 1939 the Sportsmen's Club was planning a ski area north of town with a 3,000-foot lift; an old form of recreation was showing new potential. Hunting and fishing took on an importance born of a need to supplement the family's food supply: no longer were they merely sports. As a result, poaching increased, and game wardens made sweeps through the area. In December 1940, they captured five men and charged them with illegal possession of elk, venison, and a beaver hide.

At the telephone office, the voice of "central" disappeared with the installation of dial phones in 1940. Another "old favorite" remained unchanged, however; the curfew bell rang for the children at 8 p.m. in the winter, 9 p.m. in the summertime. Children, as always, had to learn some of the other cruel lessons of life, such as not putting one's hands into the clothes wringer. Three little ones injured themselves, painfully, if not seriously, in one week in March 1935 while testing out mother's machine. When Henry Garcia shot and killed Joe Rodriquez the year before, the community talked about it for weeks; crime was generally limited to petty offenses.

Crowding the list of local heroes was an unidentified dog. One of numerous ones lounging around the town. He became an unintentional hero by tripping a frantic father who was running for the doctor's office with his baby in his arms. The little fellow had swallowed a stove bolt that became stuck in his throat, and the resulting crash dislodged the bolt, panicked the pooch, and sprained the shoulder of the distraught father. All turned out well in the end.

The business district stayed about the same size throughout these years, though individual ownerships changed. The depression hurt businessmen, and the *Pilot* returned to an old theme when it advised its readers in December 1934 to trade with their local merchant: "Your best friend when you need him most." It was deemed especially important to trade at home where dollars went to help pay taxes, educate children, make work for others, and "build your city." "Let us see that your dollars circulate in our home community."

The UMW played a role in Crested Butte as well as at the Big Mine. Their July 4, 1938, picnic featured a "delicious" lunch of barbecued lamb, enjoyed by the large crowd present; nonmembers could only drool over what they were missing. When a little extra money became available for entertainment, the Princess Theatre offered everyone a couple of hours of relaxation. No movie was more eagerly anticipated than the box office bonanza "Gone With the Wind," which made its local debut in April 1941. For forty cents adults could be transported back to an era and a life far removed from Crested Butte.

No one had to go to the theater to witness the end of an era — the community's own past was slipping away. Some of the old landmarks were torn down, replaced by modern buildings and homes with electric outlets and other improvements. More important, the second generation of pioneers was beginning to die off. Mrs. Mary Kochevar, who had immigrated in 1889, and Mrs. Annie Busatto, who had come in the late eighties, both died on the same day in June 1931. Each was eulogized for her many contributions to the town and for help to her friends and neighbors over the years. Joseph Plutt arrived in 1909, worked at the Big Mine, and supported the UMW before falling victim to bronchial pneumonia in 1939. Word also came from the old country of the deaths of friends who had returned home, but who were fondly remembered in Crested Butte. When he died in 1941, George McWilliams was one of the last links to the pioneering days, having come in 1883. He held the record for living longest in Crested Butte — nearly fifty-eight years — much of the time working for CF&I.

What changes McWilliams had seen! They covered the entire history of Crested Butte, from hard-rock camp to coal town. He also saw the transformation of the ethnic population (clearly shown by those other old-timers, Kochevar, Busatto, and Plutt). These people had contributed more to their community than was appreciated by the new generation living and working there, who had enough troubles of their own without worrying about the past. Twentieth-century born, they were more attuned to the thirties than to the fading frontier, which looked as foreign to them as Tara and the South of "Gone With the Wind."

Abruptly, the whole world of Crested Butte folks, old and young, narrowed down to one day and one place: December 7, 1941, Pearl Harbor. Few, if any, had ever before heard of this naval station, nor could they point to it on a map. After the "date that will live in infamy," the name and place would evoke memories of that chilly Colorado December morning that changed their lives.

Portents of war had become increasingly evident as the country prepared itself for that possibility. In growing numbers, Crested Butte boys began to volunteer for military service as early as 1939, perhaps more because it offered job training and a steady salary than for patriotic duty. Then in 1940, Selective Service entered the scene, and local young men were drafted into service. In January 1941, a "Soldier Boys Column" in the *Pilot* allowed home folks to follow the activities of their relatives and friends. Patriotism and enthusiasm soared. Albert Rozman, after being rejected because of poor teeth, spent "around $100 of his own money" to have them fixed. As he described it, "Fellows who can't chew beans wouldn't last long in the service." He went back and passed a second physical.

The war made both an immediate and a lasting impact. Tire sales were quickly restricted to defense interests, more boys volunteered or were drafted, and war news became the only news. A shocked town had little time to contemplate the ramifications of what was happening.

Coal production had climbed to over 200,000 tons in 1940 after a short two-year slump. Because of a coal shortage that year, the mine had gone to a six-day week for a while, with the blessing of the UMW. Until 1945 a high level of production was maintained, as the miners of the Big Mine did their part to win the war. Interestingly, news from the mines declined, perhaps in the interest of wartime security, so that no information would be leaked to the enemy. One thing that did develop was a shortage of miners, forcing the closing of some of the smaller CF&I operations in order to staff the Big Mine and keep it operating. With stepped-up production the safety record of the mine was much better than average, with only two fatalities occurring.

The war also changed the pace of life in town. War news in 1942 was gloomy, which only spurred local determination to help win it. It began to look a little bit like the First World War, when enemy aliens were required to register and war-incited hatreds flared. Just the rumor that a relocation camp for Japanese-Americans and Japanese nationals from the West Coast might be established in Gunnison County spawned a vitriolic editorial in the *Pilot* on April 9, 1942: "Don't let the Japs secure a foothold in Gunnison County, in Colorado or any place in the nation." What the writer suggested doing with these unfortunate "Japrats" was to put them to work on the Alaskan Highway in properly guarded camps. After the war, they were to be shipped to Japan, "otherwise Americans will suffer for a thousand years" for not seizing this opportunity. Unlike the German miners of 1917, this enemy did not have ties to Crested Butte.

The town was soon inundated with quotas for Red Cross needs, bond purchases, and scrap drives. The first defense bond rally in January 1942 proved a great success, launched with speeches by officials of the CF&I, UMW, and other local notables. When CF&I employee Ralph Giardino purchased $3,000 worth of bonds, he was hailed as a hero. Even the municipal election took on a wartime conservation aura, when only one party entered candidates (the next year there were none). But the real news that April week was Bataan falling, while Corregidor held out (though not for long). One of the first visible signs of the wartime emergency besides the draft was the movement of people to the West Coast for work in high-paying defense plant jobs. In Crested Butte, as elsewhere in Colorado, this exodus depleted the work force in a way not known before.

By 1943 Civil Defense was on the alert to prevent trouble and prepare for a possible attack, a far-fetched threat to the Elk Mountains. Of more importance, it organized volunteers for forest fire fighting, though the motive was that the Japanese were reportedly sending incendiary balloons toward America. Victory gardens did not produce any better than in 1917; neither the climate nor the growing season had moderated.

Rationing became a fact of life, as did war news, which improved steadily as the months went by. The "Boys in Service" column kept track of local soldiers, from England to Arabia to the Far East, telling of their promotions, medals, transfers, wounds, and deaths — or the equally dreaded "Missing in Action." Crested Butte could not hope to escape its share of war dead. By Christmas 1944, victory could be sensed. Advertisements in the *Pilot* that season expressed the traditional greetings and went a step farther: "Be thankful for the many blessings God has bestowed upon us and hope for Victory in 1945; among the things for which our boys are fighting is the right to celebrate Christmas in the traditional American way." And, finally, "We express the season's greetings to all men and women in uniform and their families and wish them God speed and a safe return home."

The year 1945 could not pass fast enough for those who only wished the war over and their loved ones returned home. President Roosevelt died in April, and Crested Butte mourned along with the rest of the nation. Flags were lowered to half mast and all businesses closed during the funeral out of "reverence" for the man. Germany surrendered, and the country was halfway home. The paper missed the significance of the first atomic bomb drop — it was pushed off the front page by a "terrific" cloudburst, which almost wiped out Marble. Then came the headline all had been waiting for: "JAPS QUIT: WAR IS OVER: NATION IS SETTLING DOWN."

CHAPTER 7

The King is Dead

1945-1952

T he war was over, victory won, and the long-anticipated tomorrow of peace was at hand. Crested Butte and the rest of the United States turned their attention to the post-war era with confidence that it would be better than yesterday. For Crested Butte, that prosperous tomorrow never quite came.

At the age of sixty-five, the community lacked the faded glamour of gold and silver camps. Crested Butte had never been much more than a coal town, which held few attractions for outsiders. Muriel Sibell Wolle, that irrepressible Colorado mining camp enthusiast, saw it with an artist's eyes. She came to sketch and listen to old-timers tell what had happened here and in the district. Her impressions and a brief history filled a couple of pages of *Stampede to Timberline*, including this description:

> *Crested Butte is still a coal town, its streets gray with coal dust and its houses somber in color, yet behind many windows blossoming plants flaunt splashes of color or lace curtains shut out the drab view of other somber homes. There are few trees and the grayness is relieved only by pocket-sized gardens overflowing with delphinium and other native plants.*

She captured in words and drawings the gentle demise of a dream. Unintentionally, she pointed out why few others followed her to this town and its Big Mine.

The post-war era was launched brightly with the encouraging forecast that the relaxation of gas rationing would bring an "additional swarm of vacation-bound tourists." They came to Colorado and to the Gunnison Country, but Crested Butte's few attractions and isolation compared unfavorably to the others. The community still relied on the Big Mine for its major source of income.

Looking back over twenty years of married life at Crested Butte, Esta Gibson recalled that raising children was easy because one always knew where they were. "All families in town took care of each other that way, it was a big family." Crested Butte was a "real community" and everyone "got along great; whenever one went to parties, all were involved." There were no strangers in town, everyone was accepted.

The ever-popular dances continued to the end of the coal mining days, with polkas predominating. Mrs. Gibson said most of the time they would dance until 2:00 or 3:00 in the morning, take up a collection to keep the band playing, then go for breakfast and come back to continue dancing into Sunday. Parties and polkas could never completely mask the essentially dangerous nature of mining. She always worried about her husband in the mines: "All miners' wives do." Esta Gibson stayed up until her husband John came home, usually passing the time sewing or knitting.

Local life continued to be recorded in a column or two of news in the Gunnison-based *Pilot*. Interest centered on the schools and their students and the comings and goings of local folks. Other items came along now and then: the school carnival, the posters for poppy day, the Pep Club's motoring to Gunnison for a basketball game (the Rangers usually met defeat there), and graduation. News of mining and Main Street took a backseat. A typical column, such as the one of January 8, 1948, might include stories about a Rebekah Lodge installation, the annual firemen's ball, the monthly meeting of the Pine Tree Club, illnesses, injuries, a local boy home on furlough, and another one going off to the University of Denver to enroll in college.

Crested Butte was "just a nice homey little town ... a nice town to live in," said Ruth Chappell, whose husband was a forest ranger there from 1943 to 1956. She provided some insights into the community and its people of a generation and more ago.

Families were very much tied in with their own families — sons, daughters, grandchildren. Very strong family ties existed, also very strong church affiliation.

It took a little doing to get accustomed to Crested Butte. It took a little while to get used to the winters, and it took a little doing to get used to the people. I felt at the time [1943] they were very distant, but found out afterwards if you ever once broke through and got acquainted, you had a friend for life.

The women were such marvelous cooks; I think they must have spent most of their time right in the kitchen [Ruth especially remembered the nut bread made by the Eastern Europeans, called "potica"].

There was a nice filling station with a big potbellied stove in the back where the men gossiped worse than any bunch of women you ever hear. The men all holed up around the potbellied stove.

Even as a family not tied directly to the coal industry, the Chappells were aware of the union and its strength. "The union was active," she said, "so active that there was a little girl who lived across the street from us; she must have been in the fourth or fifth grade. Someone asked her once who the president of the United States was, and she said John L. Lewis. That's how much impression he'd made on her."

Finally, Mrs. Chappell smiled when she recalled the winters, which entailed an "awful lot of snow shoveling." She described them this way:

After you got used to the winter, it was fun; it really was fun living in that snow. Our daughter absolutely loved it. All kids do. It took a lot of shoveling even to hang the clothes on the line. Our neighbors and I did more visiting,

I think, out in the street over our snowshovels than we did
any other time.

The only thing that bothered Ruth was the claustrophobia created when snow from the roof met the snow from the ground; then she shoveled away until the light came through the windows once more.

For those who believed omens foretold the future, the community offered a variety from which to select. The previously cited gossipy tidbits fortified the contentions of those who felt life had resumed its usual pattern. The optimists, who assumed times were getting better, could point to the painting of the Catholic Church and rectory in 1948 and a new sidewalk being laid in front of both. Even more encouraging was the 1948 town election, the first one since 1942. The Independent Party triumphed decisively over the Taxpayer Party, winning five of the six trustee positions and the mayor's chair. That same year, the Democrats won almost as overwhelmingly in Crested Butte's national election. The pessimists, who concluded times were not all that good, could point to the sudden demise of the *Pilot* in July 1949.

The town could only mirror signals coming off the hill where the miners labored, digging and hauling coal to the surface as they had for years. Clues from the Big Mine gave a fairly accurate indication of what was going on, and it was not good.

Production, which stayed over the 200,000-ton level during the war, diminished steadily in the years following; by 1951 it had sunk to the 70,000 range. The first to be affected were the single miners, always the most transient group. They left and did not come back for the next season. The work force continued to decline, though not as rapidly, indicating that the ton-per-man-per-day ration was dropping faster than the total tonnage – not good if CF&I planned to keep the old mine going. This economic fact raised the price of coal and dimmed prospects even more.

The outlook for the company looked grim. Its mine, now fifty-plus years old – situated on one of the few narrow gauge lines remaining in Colorado, far from markets and with production costs creeping up – had little to offer. Labor disputes in 1949 and 1950 further deteriorated company/worker relations and intensified cost problems. The Colorado Fuel & Iron again warned it would quit operating unless the strikes ceased, the assumption being that it meant every word of that warning.

During the last years of the forties, CF&I continued its now familiar role. Inspectors appeared periodically and other employees, such as painters and carpenters, came over from Pueblo to work on company property at the mine and town. CF&I's impact remained, as it had been, quiet but pervasive.

As the 1950s got underway, the day of decision came for the Big Mine and the coal town nestled at its feet. America caught up in the cold war against communism and the hot war in Korea took little notice of what was happening at Crested Butte. The world had literally passed this town by, and its fate held no interest for Americans now attracted to that new wonder, the television set. The world of today could be brought into their living rooms, and Crested Butte was not part of that world.

It was in the summer of 1952, on a warm August day, that the Big Mine shipped its last load of coal. Crested Butte was finished as a coal town. The chapter of its history that had opened in the frontier days of 1880 had ended. A revival seemed doubtful at that moment and has remained so ever since.

The end, when it came, was not unexpected. Krizmanich and Sporcich agreed that they had a pretty good idea it was going to happen. Little new equipment had been put into the mine during the previous five or six years, and production had declined. Somrak pointed to the fact that gas and oil had cut into coal's market. The closing was eased by CF&I's offer to the miners of jobs in Pueblo or Trinidad, with a year's option on the offer. Meanwhile the company paid the men's insurance premiums. Most of the people left, some overnight, "never said goodbye, go to hell, or anything."

Coal Production in Crested Butte
(tons)

Year	Tons	Year	Tons
1880	unknown	1917	139,184
1881	3,185	1918	143,873
1882	45,500	1919	114,991
1883	63,538	1920	134,299
1884	47,524	1921	95,255
1885	79,914	1922	74,851
1886	102,918	1923	74,541
1887	161,390	1924	68,443
1888	144,426	1925	92,428
1889	150,301	1926	120,137
1890	167,377	1927	103,708
1891	160,377	1928	83,998
1892	103,981 (est.)	1929	112,588
1893	154,788	1930	150,747
1894	121,999 (est.)	1931	127,035
1895	156,164	1932	140,671
1896	174,878	1933	152,570
1897	203,154	1934	154,578
1898	233,906	1935	178,167
1899	216,743	1936	247,826
1900	285,889	1937	280,054
1901	271,277	1938	178,884
1902	232,448	1939	190,797
1903	212,729	1940	214,316
1904	171,486	1941	284,552
1905	179,503	1942	240,822
1906	181,313	1943	210,019
1907	142,728	1944	200,351
1908	105,335	1945	161,364
1909	125,455	1946	142,683
1910	107,817	1947	140,760
1911	107,255	1948	125,969
1912	116,788	1949	108,900
1913	124,114	1950	103,695
1914	0	1951	70,751
1915	10,926	1952	32,984
1916	102,960		

Coke Production in Crested Butte
(tons)

1880	unknown		1900	84,154
1881	454		1901	68,844
1882	6,291		1902	62,720
1883	17,488		1903	57,485
1884	11,770		1904	57,990
1885	20,106		1905	45,910
1886	29,035		1906	54,429
1887	41,047		1907	43,210
1888	42,730		1908	14,727
1889	42,858		1909	28,818
1890	44,521		1910	24,655
1891	43,910		1911	21,003
1892	51,879		1912	19,612
1893	39,793		1913	19,415
1894	37,540		1914	0
1895	39,793		1915	0
1896	50,440		1916	0
1897	70,013		1917	19,380
1898	71,547		1918	19,534
1899	54,178		1919	0

Eighty Years of Population Records

Year	Crested Butte	Gunnison	Gothic	Irwin
1880	census taker ignored	888	949	1,123
1885	754	1,427	158	178
1890	857	1,105	48	45
1900	988	1,200	50	92
1910	904	1,026	0	65
1920	1,213	1,329	0	9
1930	1,251	1,415		
1940	1,145	2,177		
1950	730	2,770		
1960	289	3,477		
1970	372			
1980	959			
1990	878			
2000	1529			

Somrak said it for them all: "The mining days at Crested Butte were both hard, tough, rough times and also some of the best days that we had in our lives." He worked at dismantling the mine, salvaging what CF&I wanted from above and below ground. Finally, in November 1952, he and thirteen others finished their last day and an era ended. Johnny and his wife were among those who stayed to see what the future would bring.

Several factors brought coal mining to this finale, done in, so to speak, by its two long time allies, the CF&I and the Denver and Rio Grande. Each blamed the other, in part, for what happened. The railroad asked permission to remove its tracks after the CF&I revealed its intention of closing the Big Mine. The Crested Butte spur line had been operating at a steadily mounting deficit recently, and the D&RG was glad to be able to wriggle out from underneath it. Crested Butte contributed two-thirds of what freight moved along the Gunnison line anyway, so the entire Marshall Pass segment was closed. Once the main line of the D&RG when opened in 1881, this line lost over half a million dollars for the railroad from 1950 to 1952. The Denver & Rio Grande welcomed this opportunity to cut a narrow gauge link with its past, a past now an anachronism in the mid-twentieth century.

CF&I was willing to use the railroad as a scapegoat to justify abandoning an operation that had become increasingly inefficient and costly. As eager as the railroad was to get out, so too was CF&I. The cost of freighting the coal to market had risen to the point that the Big Mine's coal no longer could compete profitably. Only CF&I at Pueblo remained a major customer; the others looked to cheaper fuel closer to home. CF&I could do the same, and that doomed the Big Mine.

Other factors weighed in the final decision. The railroad fell victim to car and truck competition; as highway maintenance improved, particularly in the winter, the more direct and faster means of transportation took revenue away from the D&RG. Also, national coal sales slumped badly after the war, as the cleaner and cheaper natural gas, electricity, and oil replaced coal in homes and factories. Crested Butte's industrial problems duplicated those of the country as a whole. The repeated labor turmoil over the years had not helped to prolong the Big Mine's life. Production costs finally reached the point that any further labor difficulties would mean loss of profits.

Finally, there was not escaping the fact that the coal seams had been mined for over seventy years with the best and largest deposits now exhausted. This condition and all the other factors weighed against success. The CF&I made the decision. It dismantled the mine equipment, closed the workings, and terminated the miners. The company sold its buildings in town — the store, homes, service station, warehouse, hotel, boarding house. Some were moved out of Crested Butte, others continued to operate under new owners.

In the final analysis, despite what Crested Butte thought of as the heartless closing of the Big Mine, the Colorado Fuel and Iron had been a positive force in the life of this community. Without the company's support over the years, the town could not have maintained the size and economy to which it had grown accustomed. Jobs, wages, mining materials, and other commodities, entertainment, stores, improved hygiene — a bundle of benefits had come to Crested Butte via the CF&I. It had guided and undergirded the town's evolution from the rough-edged frontier settlement of the eighties, through the days of the immigrants' melting pot, to the stability of the 1930s and 1940s.

There had been both high and low points in the marriage between the community and the company, with, fortunately, more blessings than battles. Crested Butte became a company town, though not the typical dismal "company town," as a result of this marriage. Here evolved an example of the best accommodation that could be made between management and workers in an isolated coal mining district. CF&I showed that it could have the interests of the district and people at heart, along with profits in the company ledger books. What happened here should not be judged by the conditions and philosophies of today or tomorrow. It should, instead, be balanced against the philosophy of those earlier years and what occurred elsewhere throughout Colorado and the United States. A fair comparison and a balanced judgment can then be made. Colorado Fuel & Iron did well by Crested Butte.

Coal mining itself changed very little from 1880 to 1952. It remained a physically demanding, dirty, dangerous occupation, one that until the very last decades continued to be relatively low-paying at Crested Butte, when all factors were considered. The only explanation for why men continued to risk their lives underground is found in the mystique of mining. Only those who have been underground and involved can understand it. To the outsider it remains incomprehensible; to the coal miner it supplied a challenge, a fascination, and a job.

The story does not end in 1952 for Crested Butte. The situation might have appeared gloomier and more uncertain than at any other previous time, but the town did not stay down for the count. The community would not go the way of Gothic and Irwin.

The *Denver Post*, a year later, on September 16, 1953, published an article on the town that was supposed to be "Colorado's newest ghost town." Although the future had looked bleak the year before, Crested Butte, with the "tough philosophy of mining men, decided to stay and fight." A resort hotel project was already underway, the highway to Gunnison had been finished as an all-weather paved road, new life was forecast for hard-rock mining, and increased advertising was promoting the "ski life." Signposts emerged for the comeback trail of skiing, tourism, and mining. Long live the new king.

Crested Butte proved too tough to die; a new future awaited the little community. Perhaps an editorial in the *Chronicle*, July 4, 1980, summed it up as well as possible:

> *Crested Butte is a microcosm of America; it is a living testament of the world's greatest experiment in democracy. But even more, it is a pledge to our forefathers; a covenant to seek new frontiers within which individuals can grow and prosper. The land can no longer be exploited and, instead, the new frontier lies within ourselves; to learn to live with our fellow human beings and our benefactor, the earth, in harmony.*

Remembering Yesterday:
A 1980s Photographic Essay

Alot of things have changed since way back then," sang Loretta Lynn in her popular song, "Coal Miner's Daughter." For her "Butcher Hollow," or for Crested Butte, they certainly have. The Crested Butte of the 1980s was not that of 1952 in spirit, attitude, or economy.

New immigrants continued to come to the beautiful valley of the Elk Mountains; with them have come renewed growth and a new outlook. Together they have changed everything they touch. An avalanche of skiers has replaced the Big Mine as the rock upon which the economy rests. Through all the changes, there remain the town and a few old-timers, the only visible reminders of a fast fading past.

The Crested Butte of yesterday has left a proud heritage — a heritage of coal mining, of coal miners and their families, of Colorado Fuel and Iron, and of the other people who struggled to make a living on what George Sibley described as "the edge-zone between civilization and winter." They succeeded, and Crested Butte is their monument.

There is glory in what they accomplished — and heartbreak, too. These were average folks who knew the joys and frustrations of the struggle to make ends meet. Unsung Americans and immigrants shared the same dream of making life better for themselves and their children, better than what they had known before and left behind. Their story is little different from most of their contemporaries, a "quiet story of ambition gently trailing off into obscurity," as Bruce Catton once wrote.

On a summer day in 1980, photographer Richard Gilbert set out to capture what remains. This is a tribute to the Crested Butte that once was and never shall be again.

Behind Rock School and across town is the site of the Big Mine.

This was once CF&I's company store.

Homes like these sheltered generations of coal miners' families.

The Kochevar Building reminds the passerby of a longtime Crested Butte family.

Two-story outhouses created a legend.

The D&RG depot.

Law and order came early to Crested Butte.

The real heart of Crested Butte's coal era, the people: A.J. Mihelich.

Frank Yelenick.

Mary Yelenick.

Johnny Somrak points to where the snow reached eighty-eight inches in 1979-80.

Croatian Hall, a remembrance of the immigrants.

The City Hall housed a lot of history in the old days.

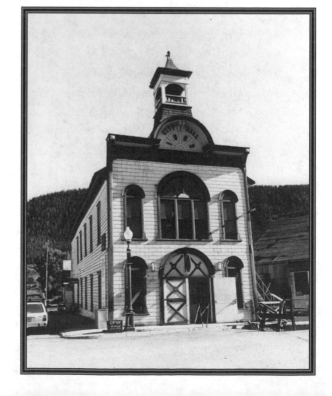

Lyle McNeill.

The Union Congregational Church speaks for values beyond materialism.

In memory of Mary C. Waters, a Crested Butte pioneer, age 6, died October 17, 1890.

Remember them all, the men and women who built and maintained Crested Butte.

Crested Butte and its namesake.

Chapter 8

From Black Gold to White Powder

1952-2005

C olorado's "newest ghost town" looked out on a new world in the early 1950s. Most of its neighboring hard rock contemporaries had gained that status long ago. Tourists looking for a souvenir of a seemingly more romantic yesteryear rummaged over them trying to imagine what long ago transpired there. So also were gone the coal mining camps that had seen so much violence, so much despair. They were sites hardly recognizable as once containing life and holding people's dreams. One time, several fading generations ago, they had all helped fuel Colorado's growth. Would Crested Butte follow their lead? Its residents had no plans to travel down that path.

They faced problems, and the problems seemed to be compounding. In 1955, the Denver & Rio Grande abandoned its line into the Crested Butte district. There was nothing diabolical in this. It was a natural reaction to the closing of the Big Mine, increased trucking, and decreased passengers and freight that left the railroad operating with a mounting deficit. Another hope, a lead, zinc, and copper mill and mining operation, had its ups and downs and failed to energize the town or district during the decade. It eventually faded away.

A 1956 visitor observed that, during the winter, Crested Butte was not a "busy place." It had only two places to eat. About all that could be done, it seemed, was talk to the natives, listen to accordion music, and eat spaghetti. One could also enjoy a drink — or two or three.

The end of coal mining cut the population of Crested Butte from 730 in 1950 to 289 ten years later. In reality, the community's population had been slowly going down since 1930, with a noticeable drop in the 1940s of slightly more than 400 people. Crested Butte had reached the nadir of its fortunes. The town struggled to maintain itself.

The main economic pillar had collapsed and the residents now needed to find some new savior that would allow their town to continue a significant life. Tourism might help, but coal mining camps had never gained the nostalgic allure of gold and silver camps. Crested Butte might have been the rare hard rock camp that became a coal camp, but that fame drew few people. The ongoing question remained. Would tourists come in large enough numbers to give the community a reason for existence?

Truly, future times were not as hopeless as they might have appeared in those years. Crested Butte sat in a spectacular and beautiful valley site — in a breathtaking mountainous neighborhood. It had also gained a needed paved road to the outside world. Outdoor activities, such as hiking, fishing, and hunting, all were available locally. With post-war Colorado enjoying a tourism boom that highlighted its mining history, Crested Butte's unusual history of hard rock and coal mining might eventually draw people. The words of the British writer H. G. Wells perfectly summarized what lay ahead for the community: "The past is but the beginning of a beginning, and all that is and has been is but the twilight of the dawn."

What offered the most promise, though, was what residents and visitors alike had discussed and cussed over the decades — snow. Wintertime Crested Butte offered that in grand abundance and for months on end. As old-timers loved to say, "Snow is the only crop that never fails around here."

People who had been to Crested Butte never forgot the snow. James Diven wrote Muriel Wolle in 1958 about his experiences fifty years earlier. A salesman for the Simmons Hardware Company, he traveled Colorado from 1902-1918. He visited the

Crested Butte region "about every five weeks" when "SNOW permitted." He continued.

You ask about Crested Butte. During my years calling there, I think I may say the 'Butte' was prosperous. Of saloons, I think there were sufficient to irrigate the populace, at least, I never heard anyone complain about 'dying' of thirst. Any mention of the 'Butte' without including SNOW would leave it incomplete. I was pretty lucky, only getting held up a few days, but a dry goods salesman with 21 trunks of samples was marooned 21 days by snow. That is — he didn't get his trunks out for 21 days. I believe he did ski out about the 14th day. In all, I carry quite happy memories of my visits in Crested Butte.

That lurked in the past; now it was the present, and a problem became a blessing. Just after the trauma of World War II ended, Colorado had soared into a new era as a major ski destination. Aspen, merely over the mountain from Crested Butte, spearheaded the development. It boomed, and its success encouraged others. The famous Tenth Mountain Division, America's ski troops who had trained near Leadville and gone on to fame during the war, helped in bringing further prominence to Colorado's ski slopes. Many of its members returned after the war and helped launch other areas over the next two decades. The state found what it had long been seeking, a key tourist attraction to fill out the year. Winter months no longer existed in a void or mountain towns in a seasonal depression.

Skiing caught on as a popular wintertime activity as never before, but not just with Coloradans and others who happened to live near the mountains. Many Americans everywhere discovered the fun and pleasure of the sport. They could now reach the slopes with an ease and comfort only imagined by earlier generations, not to mention in less time than ever before. That old bugaboo, isolation, had finally met its match. The war had shown the possibilities of air travel, and, like skiing; it came into its own after 1945. National airlines flew into Denver's Stapleton Field with increased regularity, and from there Colorado's own Frontier Airlines took them on to mountain destinations such as Gunnison, Durango, and Aspen.

The ingredients were all in place for Crested Butte. Now it remained up to determined locals to seize the opportunity. It would be a new day for them, one that offered the best chance to avoid that undesired "ghost town" status.

It started simply enough in the 1950s with a small ski area at Rozman Hill. Established and operated initially by the Western State College ski team, it provided limited lifts and runs. Typical for these years, the area had a small warming hut but not much else to offer the skiers. By the end of the 1950s, it had "outlived" its usefulness, and discussions began about how to improve on what appeared to be a promising potential. Few dreamed at that moment, however, just what skiing might become in the next decade.

Located in some of the "finest ski country in the world," according to Colorado and Gunnison County historian Duane Vandenbusche, Gunnison County and Crested Butte "inevitably would become a winter tourist mecca." What both needed was a major ski area, one that was able to compete with nearby rivals. That dream became a reality in 1961. A ski area opened two miles north of the town, and the new days dawned.

Crested Butte's evolution from a coal camp to a skiing community was well under way by the mid-sixties. The *Colorado Year Book* (1964) credited the town with a population of 300, the second largest in Gunnison County lagging far behind Gunnison's 4,000. Together, however, they represented nearly 80 percent of the county's total. Crested Butte's exciting ski area, though, caught the editor's attention.

The Crested Butte Winter Sports Area, open from Thanksgiving to mid-April, offers 23 miles of trails for skiers from beginners to experts. Facilities include a 7,500 foot gondola, a T-bar and a J-bar, a ski school, and many types of accommodations and services. Ice skating and dog sledding also are featured.

Skiing might be the "in" thing at that point, but not all of yesteryear had disappeared. The county still produced coal, more than $1,000,000 in 1963. Crested Butte's small production mattered little anymore. The community had found its new bonanza in that "damned white stuff," cursed for so many years.

Success did not come quickly or easily, despite the quality and abundance of snow. Like many other young ski areas, growing pains and financial problems continually clouded the crisp, cold skiing days in the 1960s. The situation was quaintly described as, "three lifts puttering on a hill run by a ski area teetering on the cusp of bankruptcy." The area did not make a success of its dreams. The Winter Sports Area went over the edge and into bankruptcy to become the property of its creditors, Kansas City banks.

Finally, in 1970, the Crested Butte Development Corporation purchased the property. A westernized Georgian, Howard Callaway, and his partner Ralph Walton, headed the firm, which had the strong financial backing the ski area needed. Callaway would later gain national attention, far from his ski slopes, as Secretary of the Army under Presidents Richard Nixon and Gerald Ford.

Meanwhile, Colorado skiing took off in the second half of the twentieth century and Colorado became a winter destination in ways only dreamed about earlier. Large ski resorts were aborning and growing, and Crested Butte was determined not to be left behind. Vandenbusche, who not only studied the area but skied it, wrote about the early years of the 1970s.

The new company immediately launched a vigorous campaign to transform the Crested Butte region into a giant year-round recreation area. New lifts were added, additional trails cut, and over $20,000,000 was spent for new facilities, advertising, land development, and environmental requirements. The Crested Butte ski area soon acquired a national reputation and people from all over the United States came to ski in the champagne powder snow of the quaint, old mining region.

Old it might have been, but "quaint" helped sell it, along with the beautiful location and "champagne powder" snow. The town still looked well-seasoned, and the discerning visitor could see that it had once been a coal camp, though it was now slipping into its declining years. The buildings looked old, with a recently painted structure a rarity and new construction even scarcer. Its homes and store buildings reflected what Crested

Butte once looked like, and the town still had one of those famous two-story outhouses. Crested Butte had none of the glitz and glamour that had come to another old and tired mining camp, Aspen, but potentially it could gain preservation— or, at least, repair and paint.

Despite such a melancholy appearance, underneath the surface there sparked a revived spirit. The ski area offered a potential that had not been sensed since the exciting days of the late nineteenth century. This reawakening showed in another way: People had regained their faith in Crested Butte. The population jumped by nearly 600 folks in the 1970s, rising to 959 in the 1980 census.

Progress did not come without problems and heartache. Already some long time residents were moving on as old friends and old ways disappeared. Property values started to creep up (a good time to sell), but so did taxes. New people and new lifestyles arrived, and more were on the way. These people had no ties to and little memories of the coal mining days and ways. Some had money, some did not, and all were strangers to the old Crested Butte. The time might be coming when old-times could not afford to live there or would not want to be a part of the new Crested Butte and its changing ambiance. It happened to Aspen, Georgetown, Telluride, and Breckenridge, as they were transformed from decaying mining communities into tourist and/or skiing meccas.

Conflict raised its head as some of the remaining old-timers squared off against the newcomers over a variety of issues. One of the most intriguing was the "dog problem." The latter had dogs and the former were "desirous of striking a blow" against these "strange people" to whom the roaming dogs belonged. The newcomers felt, as George Sibley wrote in his *Crested Butte Primer*, that it was their "god-given right" to let their dogs run free and do their thing. The city government spent hours trying to develop an equitable dog leash law, but to no avail. A cultural, generational, and philosophical gap separated the two groups, and for some it would never be bridged.

Crested Butte evolved in the 1960s. By the start of the seventies, it had "lodges, inns, and chalets, some of which are open all year." It combined the old and the new with sports and curio shops and "reminders of its mining past in bars, mine shafts, and the old town hall."Tourists, youthful sojourners, and skiers — not coal miners and their families — now walked the streets and patronized the stores.

Prosperity came for the ski area while the town wrestled with its future. By the end of the 1970s, Crested Butte had reached a 260,000 skier-days plateau, and expansion raced in full swing. A significant boom appeared near at hand. The incorporation of a new town, Mount Crested Butte, in 1973 strongly showed this. Located across the valley, with no ties to the past, it looked only to the future. Gunnison County had not seen the organization of a new community in anything but the oldest residents' memories. Not silver nor gold had given Mount Crested Butte birth, but "white gold" and the prospects of a brighter tomorrow and of future growth and prosperity. Long-time residents saw only another sign of the changing times.

Even the Colorado Fuel and Iron Company, which still owned land surrounding the town, had ideas of tapping into this new bonanza. The company looked at building a ski area on Gibson Ridge and Mount Axtell, west and south of Crested Butte. That dream, like many others in these boom ski years, never saw the light of day.

For "mountain high" success to happen, it would take the combination of several factors, all of which Crested Butte appeared to have. These included excellent snow, easy to challenging ski runs, a solid financial base, innovative owners, and nearby airfields (close anyway) at Gunnison and a little farther away at Montrose. In addition, better state and federal highway systems helped, as they did for every ski area. For the skiers, more and better accommodations, restaurants, and nighttime entertainments were coming. Add to this some regional and national publicity about what Crested Butte had hidden away in its valley and mountains, and success seemingly loomed as never before. How could visitors not enjoy their stay?

Tourists did start to come and enjoy Crested Butte, its scenery, and its skiing. Then suddenly the mining world crashed the party. The old coal mining town, now reinventing itself as a ski and tourist community, found its mining past catching up with the future in the 1970s and into the '80s. Not coal this time drew the miners, but molybdenum used in electrical wiring, missile and aircraft parts, and steel alloys. Nearby Crested Butte had a whole mountain of it, the beautiful Mount Emmons. The year was 1977.

The international mining company, American Metals Climax, planned to open a mining operation to tap the immense deposit. AMAX had gained its fame and fortune from mining the same metal at the Colorado town of Climax near Leadville and then opened the Henderson Mine near Empire, in the central part of the state. Climax emerged as Colorado's major mining operation in the previous generation and gained recognition as the world's largest molybdenum producer. The visitors going over Fremont Pass could see its huge open pit operation that gutted Bartlett Mountain, and they, at least, could grasp an understanding of a large-scale, modern mining operation. This was no "jackass" prospector development of days gone by.

By the late 1970s, AMAX showed why it was an international corporation. It mined tungsten, lead, zinc, potash, copper, nickel, and coal in the United States and North America, and produced oil and natural gas, tungsten, iron, cadmium, lead, and copper world wide. Gold and silver were by-products.

Old Crested Butte would have cheered such progress with its jobs, development, tax money, and general economic windfall, but old Crested Butte lived no more. New Crested Butte manifested much more environmental consciousness and concern about "quality of life," as the newcomers defined it — nature, mountains, vistas, and no pollution of any sort. Ecology and environment, unfamiliar words to the older generation, represented gospel to the younger set and the new Crested Butte residents who had not arrived because of mining. In fact, they wanted nothing to do with it.

The battle, as it unfolded in the 1970s, became one for the heart and soul of Crested Butte. It pitted development and profit against lifestyle. From the Crested Butte folks' view, it reminded one in a small way of Winston Churchill's challenge to the British people in June 1940: "We shall not flag or fail. We shall go on to the end."

AMAX's plans for the Mount Emmons project matched the size of the mineral deposit. It would require 2,000 construction workers to get the project underway, 1,400 miners to dig out the "moly," new and improved roads, mills, and a tailings pile that might become a man-made mountain. Music to the ears of old-timers, it promised a revival of days gone by combined with the new world of skiing. Crested Butte never before had seen such potential.

Those opposed to the development and who dreaded the pressures of rapid growth, which would come with such mineral expansion, worried about the impact on the local environment and the potential of air, water, and land pollution from machines, trucks, mining, general operations, and growth. What would happen to the quality of life that they sought in this valley and its quaint coal mining town? Most of all, they wanted to avoid what had happened to towns that faced such gigantic mining operations and lost their way. They pointed to a classic example, Rock Springs, Wyoming, that had simply been overwhelmed in neither a pleasant nor progressive way by large scale coal mining.

The opponents also feared speculation. In the first two years of the Mount Emmons project, land prices within Crested Butte more than doubled. Residents blamed speculators "from both coasts" trying to make a killing. That had happened before. All they had to do was peek over the mountain and look at Aspen. Such a boom would be the epilogue for the town and country they loved and hoped to preserve.

Crested Butte's city council, at a meeting attended by some 250 people in February 1979, voted unanimously to ask AMAX to stop the Mount Emmons project, until "it can come up with a less imposing plan." Said Mayor W. Mitchell, "I feel the public has a right to decide what is in their best interests." He went on to affirm that "Crested Butte is more valuable to this nation as a stable community in one of the really beautiful recreation areas as yet undestroyed by man," than as a new mine and mining operation. That hit the basic issue, a simple one, "environment vs. development," yet it was complex to resolve

To answer mounting criticism, AMAX explained even more of its plans in April 1979. They planned to build the mill and tailings disposal complex midway between Crested Butte and Gunnison and construct an ore conveyance facility from mine to mill. The company claimed the mountain would not "cave in afterward as some critics charge." While that had happened at Climax, the ore there existed near the surface; it occurred 1,200 feet down in Mount Emmons. Nor would there be run off pollution from the tailing site. The company planned an up-to-date system to avoid that threat.

To allay further concerns, the company planned to construct a road to bypass Crested Butte. The main traffic artery would go over Ohio Pass from Gunnison to the mine and mill. AMAX anticipated most of the miners would live in and commute from Gunnison. While admitting the project would have a "major effect on Gunnison County," the main growth would be in the town of Gunnison which "generally favored development," according to the company in a *Denver Post* article of February 22, 1979.

Crested Butte, which one writer degradingly described as "not much of a town really," (one can imagine local reaction to that!) gained national attention. National newspapers and magazine articles brought further notice to the community and the company. Crested Butte gained attention and found itself in the news as never before. The community gained sympathy in what appeared to be an unequal fight, while the company's image outside the industry suffered.

It had suddenly become a "dramatic example of the crunch between national energy and mineral demands and fragile local environments." The town had turned into a battleground, testing new ideas against old ones. One writer pointed out that it was a "confrontation between a former mining town now inhabited primarily by Easterners, who moved to the mountain valley for its tranquility" and a modern industrial giant that threatened that quality.

In a sense, the struggle resembled the old biblical fight of David vs. Goliath. In AMAX's corner sat federal, state, and some county authorities. Even Prunes, the burro, that spokesman of the industry, brayed into the cacophony. "I'm lucky, my food is grass and bark and leaves. No bureaucrat can regulate their growth, or prices." Not satisfied with that, he blared, "If old-time miners had been forced to replant the trees and restock the trout streams like today, they'd never have made it!" Then Prunes ended with a none-too-gentle suggestion for bumper stickers: "Ban Mining. Let the Bastards Freeze to Death in the Dark."

Norm Blake, director of the Colorado Division of Mines, echoed Prunes. "A lot of people now living in Crested Butte waited until old miners were starved out and then bought their homes at rock-bottom prices. Now there is a chance to put something back there that would produce something besides broken bones of the ski industry."

Crested Butte supporters tied the fight into the growing national environmental awareness and movement. For them it was preservation of natural beauty, concern for the total environment, and maintenance of the quality of life, all of these defined as their lifestyle. They believed, without question, that right and the future were on their side. Mining threatened everything they valued and it would not last, eventually leaving behind a heritage of exploitation and degradation.

The conflict became bitter, leaving AMAX in a quandary. Rather than trying simply to overwhelm all opposition, it took a more conciliatory approach. From the start, the company displayed "corporate sensitivity" and negotiated cautiously with Crested Butte; but meetings to present plans, express views, and hear out arguments deteriorated into stormy scrimmages.

Counterattacking with its best artillery, AMAX met with various county, state, and federal agencies and spent hundreds of thousands of dollars on surveys of cultural resources; reviews of historic districts; studies of water resources, wildlife, fish, vegetation, and soils; and statements on environmental impacts. Never before had the people, the area, the flora, and the fauna been so carefully studied and so thoroughly discussed.

Alarmed activists and articulate residents continued to fight in an effort to preserve their town and lifestyle. The battle raced right on into the 1980s, with AMAX promising to make this a precedent-setting, environmental-versus-mining project. Opponents at Crested Butte doubted the benevolent intent and purpose of any and all of the company's plans. Crested Butte had become Colorado's most publicized environmental battleground.

In the company's 1981 annual report, AMAX indicated the tide was turning and turning against AMAX.

> . . . *development was slowed down at AMAX's Mount Emmons molybdenum project in Colorado, where estimates indicate 155 million tons of mineralized material averaging 0-.44 percent molybdenum disulfide. Mine development, which would require substantial capital investment and is subject to obtaining necessary environmental permits, was planned to begin in 1982 but has been postponed for at least two years.*

In the end, AMAX retired from the fight in 1983 and declared it was writing off the project. The mine "is just an expense we'd rather not have." Depressed molybdenum prices, a glutted market, low demand, and world competition made the Mount Emmons mine unrealistic and unneeded. To carry on the conflict would have been time consuming and costly, gaining more unfavorable publicity for AMAX. Such counter productive measures would not have pleased stockholders, who had already seen the company go through several bad financial years and the closing or downsizing of some of its other molybdenum mines.

So AMAX retired after spending about $155 million — from 1977 into 1982 — on the Mount Emmons project. It did not completely withdraw. It continued to hold onto its property, and many feared it was awaiting a better molybdenum price to renew the struggle. The company reported in 1983: "The changes affecting the mining industry today are more fundamental, more dynamic and in some respects, more sweeping than we have ever seen." A year later, stockholders were told, "AMAX is taking the necessary steps to be among the most efficient and low-cost producers in its continuing businesses — paring operating expenses, trimming cost capacity and selling assets not vital to the Company's future." Crested Butte was one of those "not vital" assets.

Crested Butte had won, but not without a price and problems. Many of the newcomers who opposed the mine and AMAX drifted on to other jobs and interests, leaving the town behind. They also left behind some embittered old-time residents who remembered the mining heritage and hoped for a revival. Said one, "I'm not surprised, not in the least. They treated the town like a toy." With continued optimism, though, most of the remaining locals looked to the future and the new Crested Butte.

Certainly, there were heroes in this fight, but not necessarily villains. AMAX possessed one of the nation's best environmental records and had an outstanding environmental department. In its operations elsewhere in Colorado, the company had spent millions of dollars cleaning up environmental problems that had come from an earlier age, in addition to its own modern operations. All of that mattered little during the Mount Emmons fight.

Yet Mount Emmons and its molybdenum refused to die. If a cat has nine lives, this project nears that pace. In the summer of

2005, molybdenum broke the $30 per pound price barrier and reports surfaced that the U.S. Energy Corporation "aggressively" was seeking financing to develop a mine, guess where! A spokesman for the company told the *Crested Butte News* that the "only sure things is that mining would be scaled down from what was envisioned 25 years ago." He also pointed out that mining had become "much more environmentally friendly."

Crested Butte folks had been down this road before. Many variables had to fall into place before such talk became more than simply just that. Many issues had to be resolved, the price of molybdenum had to stay high, and locals would have to change their attitudes about mining. One or more of these seemed impossible if, as Patrick Henry declared, "I know no way of judging of the future but by the past."

The ski area, meanwhile, continued expansion with Ralph Walton guiding its destiny. Eventually, the company invested more than a million dollars in the area, which included thirteen new lifts. It also promoted Mount Crested Butte, where the firm had investments. That did not gladden hearts across the valley.

When Walton finally retired in 2001, he was "one of the elder statesman" in the Colorado ski industry. By the new century, the days of private ski area ownership had become a rarity. Skiing, as a *Denver Post* reporter (February 15, 2001) wrote, "…is more of a business than a sport" and the days "are gone" when people "who simply loved to ski" operated ski areas. Callaway and Walton tried to sell Crested Butte four years before, during a "resort buying frenzy that saw corporate consolidation of resorts across the country." Nothing had come of that effort, however.

As he stepped aside, Walton was hailed for transforming the resort. He and Callaway "had rolled up their sleeves and begun a transformation still under way today." They had basically turned a "sleepy little town into a viable ski area." For himself, Walton remarked, "I've had a heck of a good time."

Not everyone in Crested Butte agreed with just how beneficial the ski corporation had been to their community. For much of the nineties, times had not been particularly good, as larger and more attractive ski areas took patrons away. This hurt the community's tourism and revenue. The locals also worried about exactly what the company planned to do with expansion. A big uproar in 1993-94 over preserving ranch land, open spaces, view corridors, wetlands, and access to the wilderness, forced the ski area to reconsider its priorities.

Affordable housing, as in every other ski town in the state, caused additional strong feelings and lengthy discussions. Workers found it difficult to find low-cost housing or decent rentals they could reasonably afford considering their wages were at the minimum level, or slightly above.

It did not help, either, to find out that management planned on "revitalizing" Mount Crested Butte, now described as an "aging" village. That, a proponent claimed, would be the catalyst for an economic renaissance down the hill, for the "funky town of Crested Butte." Being described as a "funky," second-class, hand-me-down community lying across the valley, hurt.

The company agreed to work with the community to preserve that "flair that is unique to the town of Crested Butte, where playtime is just as important as work. We'd like to keep the Crested Butte edge. It's real here, it's not like 'have a nice day, sir.' It's 'nice hat, dude.'" Still, problems existed.

Despite such encouraging talk, the days of private ownership of major ski areas, as mentioned, was drawing to an end throughout Colorado. Large corporations with "deep pockets" roared to the ascendancy in ownership and in charting the direction of the business. The Callaway and Walton families did not have the resources to match their competitors or the motivation that had driven them a generation before. Their ski area was not near a large population center, nor did it have easy access, by way of an interstate highway, to more distant large communities. Times were changing in other ways as well.

Competition from outside of Colorado hurt the state's ski areas. Skiing was not helped by the fact that five years of drought had cut winter snowfall in many Colorado mountain locations. Americans, additionally, were getting grayer and older, turning to other forms of relaxation and winter fun. The cost of a day's or week's skiing vacation had also steadily increased, cutting into the potential market. The younger generation was turning to snowboarding, which caused conflicts on the slopes about sharing runs and resulted in out-of-control skiers and boarders. All this raised questions about future days.

An end of an era came in October 2003, when the Callaway/Walton ownership sold the ski area to Vermont resort developers Tim and Diana Mueller, who bucked the trend of private ownership. Times had not been particularly prosperous for several years, when the number of skier visits plunged from a high of 550,000 back in 1997-1998 down to the mid-300,000 range. Crested Butte had suffered, as well, with the sales tax revenue dropping nearly 25 percent in the same period.

The *Denver Post*, nearly a year before, on November 24, 2002, reported that "depression shocked the local community" into realizing that "working with the ski area is more effective in preserving the town's unique appeal than battling the ski area in a fight to protect that appeal." The "vintage hamlet" wanted to "pull back to its roots," which some defined as its "rowdy image." Not wishing to compete with the big resort towns near the interstate, Crested Butte wanted to return to its "old days" of "more funk than glitz."

The new owners agreed. "If we can retain the unique qualities and amenities without becoming a sprawling area, it will become unique in the market's eyes." Well into 2005, the discussion went on about how this should or could be done. Sounding much like a generation ago, some of the dwindling number of old-timers still grumble about the recreational-based economy and their changing town. Others embrace the now quarter-of-a-century-old lifestyle and join their neighbors in enjoying the new way of life. Times have changed, however, when someone who has lived in the town for twenty years is described as a "long term" resident.

Times have changed, but yet, maybe, they have not. Helen Hunt Jackson must have smiled when the Crested Butte Chamber of Commerce and some businessmen decided that those flowers she so loved could help promote tourism. In 1985, they organized the Crested Butte Wildflower Festival. It was "dedicated to the conservation, preservation and appreciation of wildflowers."

Four years later the young festival managed to have their community legislatively designated the "Wildflower Capital of Colorado." Growth and success came, and what had been a weekend became a weeklong festival. As a *Denver Post* article, July 3, 2005, noted, the "family-friendly" festival includes a wide variety of events including walks, horse-drawn wagon and jeep tours, photography classes, instruction on creating a wildflower garden, and even college credit courses. As Jackson appreciated the beauty of the Elk Mountains, its rivers and meadows, so now will more of her spiritual descendants.

Epilogue

Anew chapter of Crested Butte's chronicle opened with a bang in the first half year of the Muellers' ownership. They announced a plan for $6.5 million in improvements for the next season, including two new chairlifts, expanded snowmaking and grooming, and remodeled base-area buildings. That, however, proved just the start. A real estate boom raced over Crested Butte and the valley. The *Denver Post* (July 5, 2004) described the frenzy.

> *. . . homeowners, developers and real estate speculators are moving aggressively in their [Muellers] shadow.*
>
> *Crested Butte area real estate values are soaring, and homes are selling at a clip that has already made 2004 the biggest year ever. New projects sprout almost daily. Last week's sale of units at the just-renovated Grand Lodge saw buyers lining up outside the hotel at 5:45 a. m. before shattering the area's one day sales record.*
>
> *And throughout the valley, new homesites are hitting the market, and old houses are getting face-lifts.*

All this overwhelmed and stretched Crested Butte's planning department. The Town Council responded by passing an emergency ordinance to limit the number of building projects "the town's staff will consider each month to eight." What all this might mean to the future would await another day. Partially what it meant, by the summer of 2005, was decision of ski area expansion to attract more families.

Meanwhile, Crested Butte eventually came to an angle of repose with its heritage of both hard rock and coal mining. The newcomers, aided by some old-timers, organized a historical society and created a historic district. Most of the surviving buildings and homes, largely frame, reflected the nineteenth and early twentieth century days and middle class styles, although, as historian Tom Noel noted, "with often fanciful restorations and additions." He went on to observe that the town "has been spared some of the intense development that has transformed Aspen, Breckenridge, and Telluride."

Some innovative planning and remodeling in the 1980s and the 1990s transformed the former mule barns into condominiums, the CF&I company store into a mini-shopping mall, and the company's boarding house into a lodge. Thus, the present found a profitable use for the past and Crested Butte's legacy lived on into the twenty-first century.

Those old homes had received new coats of paint and renovation. Preservation, despite some grumbling, became regarded with favor. The town probably in its "salad" days never looked as good as it does in the new century.

The community also changed in another way. The 2000 census found that Crested Butte had spurted from a population of 865 ten years before to 1,529, a 76.8 percent growth, and the largest total in its history. Breaking that figure down, 97.6 percent were whites and 84.6 percent being between the ages of 16-64 with less than 2 percent being older. Forty-seven point six percent owned their own homes. Those figures compared favorably with another mountain ski town, Breckenridge, which had, for example, a growth of 73.9 percent — 97.7 percent white residents and 86.8 percent between the ages of 16-64. Only 39.4 percent in Breckenridge owned their own homes, however.

Both of these communities were growing much faster than the rest of the state. They also had more white residents and were much younger. Only 64.7 percent of Colorado's population fell into the 16-64 age bracket. Over two-thirds of Coloradans owned their own homes, a much higher figure than in the mountain towns.

That striking difference in home ownership might eventually be narrowed. Finally after years of discussion construction began in the spring of 2004 on an "affordable" housing project. This common problem continually encountered by all ski towns and many popular mountain communities would hopefully be answered in Crested Butte. The Paradise Park site would feature a variety of single-family homes, duplexes and apartments.

More tourists were coming to enjoy the beautiful summer and fall days in the mountains and savor some of the local history. A more balanced seasonal economy thus emerged. Crested Butte's population gained a significant year-round income for the first time since the coal mining days.

Interestingly, Crested Butte, like other ski towns, found that the summers were getting to be "hot tourist times," with sales rising at a faster rate than winter sales. From 1999 through 2003, summer tax revenue surpassed winter in three of the five years. Where once summer proved an extra bonus to winter, the pattern seemed to be changing. What this might mean for the future posed fascinating questions.

All this was fine, but it raised a question about the future. Crested Butte lies at the end of the paved road, which during the summer means that tourists who want to travel beyond find only, at best, gravel. The suggestion to pave the thirteen-mile stretch across Cottonwood Pass to Buena Vista raised pluses and minuses. This would put Denver about an hour closer and get drivers to Interstate 70 faster. Maintaining asphalt is also cheaper than a gravel road. Other towns in the area leaned toward supporting the plan; to them it seemed like a good idea whose time had come.

Crested Butte denizens, however, were divided on the issue of paving. The essential question remained as old as ever and was seemingly simple: "How much closer it wants to get to civilization, and at what cost." The *Crested Butte News* reminded its readers, "But another cost is the loss of quiet caused by additional traffic to the area of Cottonwood Pass and Taylor Park." So there the matter rests with a decision yet to be made in the future.

Crested Butte had been evolving for more than fifty years, ever since the Big Mine closed and the coal era ended. It had never been a ghost town. Crested Butte residents proved too tough, too resilient for that epilogue. In a changing world, the newcomers had faith in their little community, faith in the future. The old-timers, who are gone now, would have understood, would have been proud that their town still persevered in the twenty-first century.

Like Mark Twain, Crested Butte can say with confidence. "The reports of my death are greatly exaggerated." Optimistically too, future Crested Butte folk will agree with the great American humorist. "Only he who has seen better days and lives to see better days again knows their full value."

It has been 125 years since the town plat was filed and Crested Butte's incorporation was completed. Each succeeding generation had its problems, successes, joys, and sorrows, as well as its community highs and lows. Throughout it all, the town persisted and survived. Now Crested Butte, its ski area, and its recreational enticements enter into another chapter of history. What that might mean only the future will tell, but, if the past serves as any guide, Crested Butte can look forward to another 125 years.

Crested Butte 2005:
A PHOTOGRAPHIC ESSAY

Crested Butte's neighbors are all gone now. All that's left of Ruby/Irwin, Gothic, Floresta, and the others are memories of a vanished West. Graveyards are the only indication that people once lived, loved, worked, and played there.

Mules and miners no longer move coal out of the ground from the Big Mine, and the smaller mines have nearly all been forgotten. Prospectors have long stopped scurrying about the mountains hoping to make a big strike. The Denver & Rio Grande has vanished into yesterday, and few people recall the days when coal was king. As the author of the 103rd Psalms once wrote, "For the wind passeth over it, and it is gone; and the place thereof shall know it no more."

Yet, Crested Butte did not share that fate. Unique in western mining history as having evolved from a silver and gold district into a thriving coal mining community, it lives on. Today, the Crested Butte resident of 125 years ago would find a few familiar things, but he or she would be amazed at the change.

Change has kept Crested Butte alive, promising an even better tomorrow. As the British poet, Edmund Spenser, noted, "But times do change and move continually."

Not much remains of the Big Mine or any of its contemporaries.

Matt Hutson

Rock School has weathered generations of students.

Matt Hutson

Croatian Hall brings back memories of yesteryear.

Matt Hutson

The false fronted building speaks to the pioneer past.

Matt Hutson

The Kochevar Building looks better today than it did for years.

Matt Hutson

Elk Avenue retains its turn-of-the-century flavor.

Matt Hutson

The heritage of the old mixes with the modern stores.

Matt Hutson

A furniture, bakery, and drugstore once occupied this block, now the businesses are aimed at tourists, skiers, and outdoor enthusiasts.
Matt Hutson

If walls could speak, what a story could be told.

Matt Hutson

Index

If you enjoyed *Crested Butte*, you may like reading these other titles from Western Reflections Publishing Co.:

Blown to Bits in the Mines: A History of Mining & Explosives in the United States

Crested Butte: A Novel

A History of Skiing in Colorado

Colorado Mining Stories

Colorado Mountain Women

Early Days on the Western Slope of Colorado

Riches to Rust: A Guide to Mining in the Old West

Silver Camp Called Creede: A Century of Mining

Mountains of Silver: Life in Colorado's Red Mountain Mining District

Silver & Sawdust: Life in the San Juans

To find out more about these titles and others, visit our web site at www.westernreflectionspub.com or call for a free catalog at 1-800-993-4490.